TENTH EDITION

Asking the Right Questions

A Guide to Critical Thinking

M. Neil Browne

Stuart M. Keeley

Bowling Green State University

PEARSON

Boston Columbus Indianapolis New York San Francisco Upper Saddle River
Amsterdam Cape Town Dubai London Madrid Milan Munich Paris Montreal Toronto
Delhi Mexico City Sao Paulo Sydney Hong Kong Seoul Singapore Taipei Tokyo

Senior Acquisitions Editor: Brad Potthoff
Editorial Assistant: Nancy C. Lee
Associate Managing Editor: Bayani Mendoza de Leon
Project Manager: Pat Brown
Marketing Manager: Sandra McGuire
Art Director: Jayne Conte
Production and Composition Services: Nithya Kuppuraj/PreMediaGlobal
Cover Designer: Karen Salzbach
Printer and Binder: Courier Westford
Cover Printer: Courier Westford

Credits and acknowledgments borrowed from other sources and reproduced, with permission, in this textbook appear on appropriate page within text.

Library of Congress Cataloging-in-Publication Data

Browne, M. Neil, 1944-
Asking the right questions : a guide to critical thinking/M. Neil Browne,
Stuart M. Keeley.—10th ed.
p. cm.
Includes index.
ISBN-13: 978-0-205-11116-9
ISBN-10: 0-205-11116-5
1. Criticism. 2. Critical thinking. I. Keeley, Stuart M., 1941- II. Title.
PN83.B785 2011
808—dc23
2011020512

1 2 3 4 5 6 7 8 9 10—*V*013—14 13 12 11

Student Edition
ISBN-13: 978-0-205-11116-9
ISBN-10: 0-205-11116-5

Exam Copy
ISBN-13: 978-0-205-11119-0
ISBN-10: 0-205-11119-X

CONTENTS

PREFACE

"I know it's good to be a critical thinker and to be able to ask lots of good questions, but I don't know what questions to ask or how to ask them." We are now on our tenth edition of a book that we wrote in response to sensing the need for providing more guidance for the process of effectively asking critical questions. Democracy works best with a public capable of critical thinking! We can be more confident of our decisions and beliefs when we have formed them only after asking critical questions.

From the beginning, our book has been a work in progress, as we continue to incorporate input from our students and from the many teachers using this book. While we continue to be immensely pleased by this book's success and the positive feedback from many readers from many countries, we cannot also help but notice the need for a greater-than-ever expansion of efforts to educate the public in "asking the right questions." Selecting which new suggestions to embrace and which to reject has become increasingly difficult. We are bombarded daily with efforts to persuade us, many of which are highly polarized and appeal much more to the emotional part of the brain than to the reasoning part. We encounter a general, immense disrespect for evidence, the sloppy use of language, and substitution of hollering for reason in so much of our public discussion. "Truthiness," or a lack of concern for the truth, becomes more and more common.

Always uppermost in our mind has been the desire to retain the primary attributes of *Asking the Right Questions*, while adjusting to new emphases in our own thought and the evolving needs of our readers. For instance, we want most of all to keep this book concise, readable, and short. Also, our experience has convinced us that the short book succeeds in the job for which it was intended—the teaching of critical-thinking questioning skills. Our experience in teaching critical-thinking skills to our students over four decades has convinced us that when individuals with diverse abilities are taught these skills in a simplified format, they can learn to apply them successfully. In the process, they develop greater confidence in their ability to make rational choices about social issues and personal issues, even those with which they have formerly had little experience.

Thus, our book continues to do a number of things that other books have failed to do. This text develops an integrated series of question-asking skills that can be applied widely. These skills are discussed in an informal style. (We have written to a general audience, not to any specialized group.)

One feature that deserves to be highlighted is the applicability of *Asking the Right Questions* to numerous life experiences extending far beyond the classroom. The habits and attitudes associated with critical thinking are transferable to consumer, medical, legal, and general ethical and personal choices. When a surgeon says surgery is needed, it can be life sustaining to seek answers to the critical questions encouraged in *Asking the Right Questions*. In addition, practicing the critical-thinking questions enhances our growth of knowledge in general and helps us better discover the way the world is, how it could be better understood, and how we can make it a better world.

Who would find *Asking the Right Questions* especially beneficial? Because of our teaching experiences with readers representing many different levels of ability, we have difficulty envisioning any academic course or program for which this book would not be useful. In fact, the first nine editions have been used in law, English, pharmacy, philosophy, education, psychology, sociology, religion, and social science courses, as well as in numerous high school classrooms.

A few uses for the book seem especially appropriate. Teachers in general education programs may want to begin their courses by assigning this book as a coherent response to their students' requests to explain what is expected of them. English courses that emphasize expository writing could use this text both as a format for evaluating arguments prior to constructing an essay and as a checklist of problems that the writer should attempt to avoid as she writes. The text can also be used as the central focus of courses designed specifically to teach critical reading and thinking skills.

While *Asking the Right Questions* stems primarily from our classroom experiences, it is written so that it can guide the reading and listening habits of almost everyone. The skills that it seeks to develop are those that any critical reader needs to serve as a basis for rational decisions. The critical questions stressed in the book can enhance anyone's reasoning, regardless of the extent of his or her formal education.

The special features of this new edition include the following:

1. We continue with think-aloud answers for early practice passages—expressing critical-thinking responses to a passage as if the reader were inside the head of a person struggling with the challenge of evaluating the practice passages. We think that "hearing" the bit-by-bit process of accepting, rejecting, revising, and organizing an answer gives the reader a more realistic picture of the actual critical-thinking process used to achieve an answer than would simply observing an answer. Here we are relying on the important metaphor of John Gardner who chastised teachers and trainers for showing learners only the cut flowers of knowledge and not the planting, weeding, fertilizing, and pruning that result in a beautiful bouquet. Also, we greatly expand the think-aloud feedback process in the student manual for the tenth edition.
2. We also emphasize the social or interactive nature of critical thinking and the real-world realty that the way in which one asks critical-thinking questions can greatly influence the value of the questioning. For example, many readers initially flexing their critical-questioning muscles with others find that not everyone welcomes the critical questioning of their beliefs. Some interactive approaches stimulate much more

satisfactory dialogues between the critical thinker and the speaker or writer than others. We suggest questioning and listening strategies to keep the conversation going rather than shutting it down. For example, critical questioning will often be brought to a quick halt by a listener's response of, "Why are you picking on me?"

3. We have inserted many new examples and practice passages to provide frequent engagement with contemporary issues and to demonstrate critical thinking's real-life value and application.
4. The tenth edition focuses on using the skills to enhance the reader's own writing and speaking. In other words, critical-thinking skills are not just applied to the arguments of someone else, but to the formative process of creating our own arguments. The new emphasis yields an important dimension to learning critical thinking.
5. We have added more illustrations at key sections of the book to offer the advantages of visual learning for some readers.

Companion Website

An expanded student Companion Website can be found at http://www.pearsonhighered.com/browne. This invaluable study tool offers self-testing opportunities, many additional practice exercises, some with and some without feedback from the authors; and includes lengthy practice passages with think-aloud feedback. In addition, the Website provides examples of the application of the entire set of critical-thinking questions to very lengthy essays. Also, we have added samples of "polished" lengthy essays so that students can view critical thinking excellence in action.

Instructor's Manual

An Instructor's Manual provides comprehensive assistance for teaching with Asking the Right Questions. Instructors may download this supplement at http://www.pearsonhighered.com/ or request a printed copy through their local Pearson representative.

This tenth edition owes special debts to many people. We wish to acknowledge the valuable advice of the following Prentice Hall reviewers: William Brugger, BYU – Idaho; Preston Coleman, Gainesville State College; Jeffrey Easlick, Plymouth State University; E. Kay Harris, University of Southern Mississippi; Christine Kirsch, ITT Technical Institute; Fran Rancourt, Plymouth State University; and Carla Thomson, Palomar College.

While our students are always a major source of suggested improvements, a few distinguished themselves in that regard. The tenth edition benefited from the especially valuable assistance of Bethany Nanamaker, Lauren Biksacky, and Jill Hagerman.

M. Neil Browne

Stuart M. Keeley

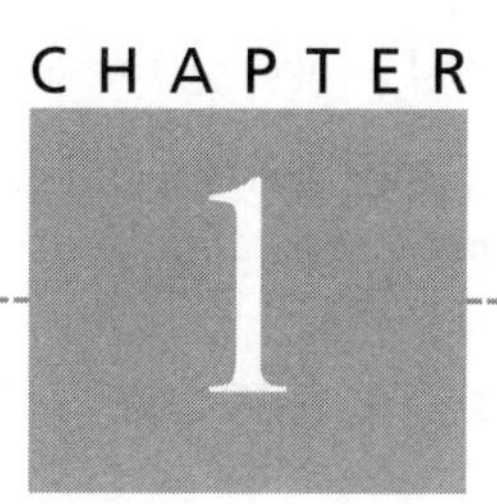

The Benefit and Manner of Asking the Right Questions

INTRODUCTION

Dozens of film experts are eager to tell us which movies to see and which to avoid. But which of these opinions should we follow? Which film authority provides the most convincing reasons on a regular basis to support her conclusion?

The authors of this book are film fanatics, but, like you, we do not want to see every film. Deciding which film to see is hard work. To make the task easier, we often use one of our favorite Web sites, http://www.rottentomatoes.com.

However, as soon as you arrive at that site, you quickly notice that film experts almost never agree among themselves. This experience is a metaphor for much of life. Doctors, legislators, architects, plumbers, and detectives all disagree among themselves about the proper course of action in particular circumstances. How are we, the consumers of opinions, to respond? The book you are about to read contains the best answer we know. You need to build skills and attitudes that will enable you to decide for yourself which opinions to make your own.

As a thoughtful person, you must make a choice about how you will react to what you see and hear. One alternative is to just accept whatever you read or hear; doing so automatically results in your making someone else's opinion your own. No one wants to be another person's mental slave.

A more active and impressive alternative consists of asking certain powerful questions in an effort to reach a personal decision about the worth of what you have experienced. This book is written for those who prefer the second alternative. While we will give you a lot of guidance about what questions to ask and when to ask them, for now all we want to say is that the path to reasonable conclusions begins and proceeds with questions.

CRITICAL THINKING TO THE RESCUE

Listening and reading critically—that is, reacting with systematic evaluation to what you have heard and read—requires a set of skills and attitudes. These skills and attitudes are built around a series of related critical questions. While we will learn them one by one, our goal is to be able to use them as a unit to identify the best decision available. Ideally, asking these questions will become part of who you are, not just something you studied in a book.

Critical thinking, as we will use the term, refers to the following:

1. awareness of a set of interrelated critical questions;
2. ability to ask and answer critical questions in an appropriate manner; and
3. desire to actively use the critical questions.

The goal of this book is to encourage you in all three of these dimensions.

Questions require the person being asked the question to do something in response. By our questions, we are saying to the person: "I am curious"; "I want to know more"; "help me." This request shows respect for the other person. Critical questions exist to inform and provide direction for all who hear them. In that respect, critical thinking begins with the desire to improve what we think. The critical questions are also useful in improving your own writing and speaking because they will assist you when you:

1. react critically to an essay or to evidence presented in a textbook, in a periodical, or on a Web site;
2. judge the quality of a lecture or a speech;

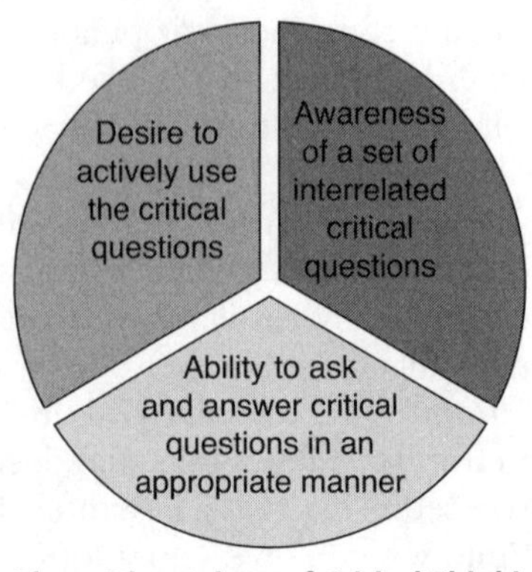

Three Dimensions of Critical Thinking

3. form an argument;
4. write an essay based on a reading assignment; or
5. participate in class.

Attention: ***Critical thinking consists of an awareness of a set of interrelated critical questions, plus the ability and willingness to ask and answer them at appropriate times.***

THE SPONGE AND PANNING FOR GOLD: ALTERNATIVE THINKING STYLES

One common approach to thinking is similar to the way in which a sponge reacts to water: by absorbing. This popular approach has some clear advantages.

First, the more information you absorb about the world, the more capable you are of understanding its complexities. Knowledge you have acquired provides a foundation for more complicated thinking later.

A second advantage of the sponge approach is that it is relatively passive. Rather than requiring strenuous mental effort, it tends to be rather quick and easy, especially when the material is presented in a clear and interesting fashion. Though absorbing information provides a productive start toward becoming a thoughtful person, the sponge approach also has a serious and devastating disadvantage: It provides no method for deciding which information and opinions to believe and which to reject. If a reader relied on the sponge approach all the time, he would believe whatever he read last.

We think you would rather choose for yourself what to absorb and what to ignore. To make this choice, you must read with a special attitude—a question-asking attitude. Such a thinking style requires active participation. The writer is trying to speak to you, and you should try to talk back to him, even though he is not physically present.

We call this interactive approach the panning-for-gold style of thinking. The process of panning for gold provides a model for active readers and listeners as they try to determine the worth of what they read and hear. Distinguishing the gold from the gravel in a conversation requires you to ask frequent questions and to reflect on the answers.

The sponge approach emphasizes knowledge acquisition; the panning-for-gold approach stresses active interaction with knowledge as it is being acquired. Thus, the two approaches complement each other. To pan for intellectual gold, there must be something in your pan to evaluate. In addition, to evaluate arguments, we must possess knowledge, that is, dependable opinions.

Let us examine more closely how the two approaches lead to different behavior. What does the individual who takes the sponge approach do when he reads material? He reads sentences carefully, trying to remember as much

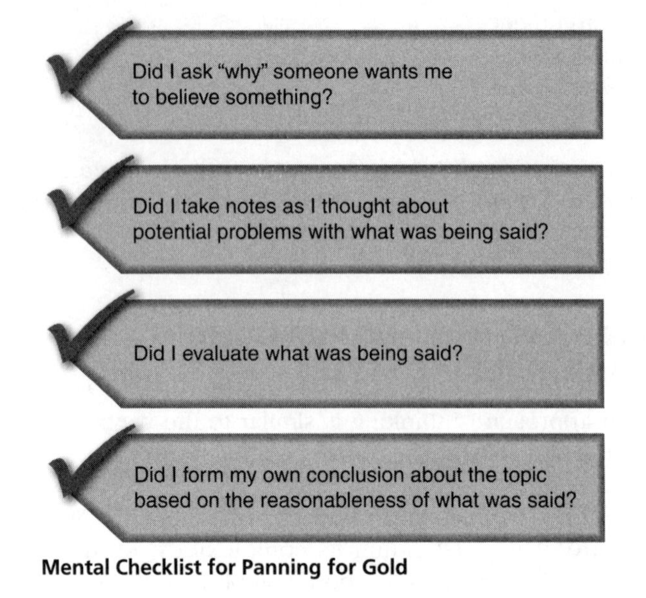

Mental Checklist for Panning for Gold

as he can. He may underline or highlight key words and sentences. He may take notes summarizing the major topics and major points. He checks his underlining or notes to be sure that he is not forgetting anything important. His mission is to find and understand what the author has to say. He memorizes the reasoning, but doesn't evaluate it.

What does the reader who takes the panning-for-gold approach do? Like the person using the sponge approach, she approaches her reading with the hope that she will acquire new knowledge. There the similarity ends. The panning-for-gold approach requires that the reader ask herself a number of questions designed to uncover the best available decisions or beliefs.

The reader who uses the panning-for-gold approach frequently questions why the author makes various claims. She writes notes to herself in the margins indicating problems with the reasoning. She continually interacts with the material. Her intent is to critically evaluate the material and formulate personal conclusions based on the evaluation.

AN EXAMPLE OF THE PANNING-FOR-GOLD APPROACH

A major enduring issue in American society concerns what kind of gun control laws we need. Let's look at one position on this issue.

> Arguments for banning guns are mostly myths, and what we need now is not more laws, but more law enforcement. One myth is that most murderers are ordinary, law-abiding citizens who kill a relative or acquaintance in a moment of anger only because a gun is available. In fact,

> every study of homicide shows the overwhelming majority of murderers are career criminals, people with lifelong histories of violence. The typical murderer has a prior criminal history averaging at least six years, with four major felony arrests.
>
> Another myth is that gun owners are ignorant rednecks given to senseless violence. However, studies consistently show that, on the average, gun owners are better educated and have more prestigious jobs than non-owners. To judge by their applications for permits to carry guns, the following are (or were) gun owners: Eleanor Roosevelt, Joan Rivers, Donald Trump, and David Rockefeller.
>
> Even if gun laws do potentially reduce gun-related crime, the present laws are all that are needed if they are enforced. What good would stronger laws do when the courts have demonstrated that they will not enforce them?

If you apply the sponge approach to the passage, you probably will try to remember the reasons that we don't need further controls on guns However, how convinced should you be by the above-mentioned reasons? You can't evaluate them until you have applied the panning-for-gold approach to the passage—that is, until you have asked the right questions.

By asking the right questions, you would discover a number of possible weaknesses in the communicator's arguments. For instance, you might be concerned about all of the following:

1. What does the author mean by "overwhelming majority" or by "typical murderer"? Is the minority still a substantial number of murderers who kill relatives in a moment of anger?
2. What does "gun owners" mean? Are they the ones who buy the kind of guns that gun control advocates are trying to ban?
3. How adequate were the cited research studies? Were the samples sufficiently large, random, and diverse?
4. What possible benefits of gun control are not mentioned? Have important studies that disagree with the author's position been omitted?
5. How many people are killed each year by handguns, who would not have been killed were such guns not available?

If you would enjoy asking these kinds of questions, this book is especially for you. Its primary purpose is to help you know when and how to ask questions that will enable you to decide what to believe.

The most important characteristic of the panning-for-gold approach is interactive involvement—a dialogue between the writer and the reader, or the speaker and the listener. You are willing to agree, but first you need some convincing answers to your questions.

The inadequacies in what someone says will not always leap out at you. You must be an *active* reader and listener. You can do this by *asking questions*. The best search strategy is a critical-questioning strategy. A powerful advantage of these questions is that they permit you to ask probing questions even when you know very little about the topic being discussed. For example, you do not need to be an expert on childcare to ask critical questions about the adequacy of day-care centers.

THE MYTH OF THE "RIGHT ANSWER"

Our ability to find definite answers to questions often depends on the type of question that puzzles us. Scientific questions about the physical world are the most likely to have answers that almost all reasonable people will accept, because the physical world is in certain ways more dependable or predictable than the social world. While we may not be absolutely certain about the precise distance to the moon or the age of a newly discovered bone from an ancient civilization, agreement about the dimensions of our physical environment is widespread. Thus, in the physical sciences, we frequently can arrive at "the right answer."

Questions about human behavior and about the meaning of our behavior are different. The causes of human behavior are so complex that we frequently cannot do much more than form intelligent guesses about why or when certain behavior will occur. In addition, because many of us care a great deal about explanations and descriptions of human behavior, we prefer that explanations or descriptions of the rate of abortion, the effects of obesity, or the causes of child abuse be consistent with what we want to believe. Hence, we bring our preferences to any discussion of those issues and resist arguments that are inconsistent with them.

Because human behavior is so controversial and complex, the best answers that we can find for many questions about our behavior will be probabilistic in nature. Even if we were aware of every bit of evidence about the effects of exercise on our mental health, we could still not expect certainty about those effects. We still need to commit to a particular course of action to prevent our becoming a "hollow man" or a "nowhere woman." But once we acknowledge that our commitments are based on probability and not certainty, we will be much more open to the reasoning of those who are trying to persuade us to change our minds. After all, we may well be wrong about some of our beliefs. We have to listen respectfully to those with whom we disagree. They just may be right.

Regardless of the type of questions being asked, the issues that require your closest scrutiny are usually those about which "reasonable people" disagree. In fact, many issues are interesting exactly because there is strong disagreement about how to resolve them. Any controversy involves more than one position. Several positions may be supported with good reasons. There will seldom be a position on a social controversy about which you will be able to say, "This is clearly the right position on the issue." If such certainty were possible, reasonable people would not be debating the issue. Our focus in this book will be on such social controversies.

THE USEFULNESS OF ASKING THE QUESTION, "WHO CARES?"

Asking good questions is difficult but rewarding work. Some controversies will be much more important to you than others. When the consequences of a controversy for you and your community are minimal, you will want to spend less time and energy thinking critically about it than about more important controversies. For example, it makes sense to critically evaluate arguments for and against the protection of endangered species because different positions on this issue lead to important consequences for society. It makes less sense to devote energy to evaluating whether blue is the favorite color of most corporate executives.

Your time is valuable. Before taking the time to critically evaluate an issue, ask the question, "Who cares?"

WEAK-SENSE AND STRONG-SENSE CRITICAL THINKING

Previous sections mentioned that you already have opinions about many personal and social issues. You are willing right now to take a position on such questions as: Should prostitution be legalized? Is alcoholism a disease or willful misconduct? Was George W. Bush a successful president? You bring these initial opinions to what you hear and read.

Critical thinking can be used to either (1) defend or (2) evaluate and revise your initial beliefs. Professor Richard Paul's distinction between weak-sense and strong-sense critical thinking helps us appreciate these two antagonistic uses of critical thinking.

Attention: *Weak-sense critical thinking is the use of critical thinking to defend your current beliefs. Strong-sense critical thinking is the use of the same skills to evaluate all claims and beliefs, especially your own.*

If you approach critical thinking as a method for defending your present beliefs, you are engaged in *weak-sense critical thinking*. Why is it weak? To use critical-thinking skills in this manner is to be unconcerned with moving toward truth or virtue. The purpose of weak-sense critical thinking is to resist and annihilate opinions and reasoning different from yours. To see domination and victory over those who disagree with you as the objective of critical thinking is to ruin the potentially humane and progressive aspects of critical thinking.

In contrast, *strong-sense critical thinking* requires us to apply the critical questions to all claims, including our own. By forcing ourselves to look critically at our initial beliefs, we help protect ourselves against self-deception and conformity. It is easy to just stick with current beliefs, particularly when many people share them. But when we take this easy road, we run the strong risk of making mistakes we could otherwise avoid.

Strong-sense critical thinking does not necessarily force us to give up our initial beliefs. It can provide a basis for strengthening them because critical examination of those beliefs will sometimes reinforce our original commitment to them. Another way of thinking about this distinction is to contrast open and closed mindedness. When my mind is open, it welcomes criticism of my own beliefs. But when my mind is closed, the beliefs I have are going to be the ones I keep.

To feel proud of a particular opinion, it should be one we have selected—selected from alternative opinions that we have understood and evaluated.

THE SATISFACTION OF PANNING FOR GOLD

Doing is usually more fun than watching; doing well is more fun than simply doing. If you start using the interactive process taught in this book, you can feel the same sense of pride in your reading and listening that you normally get from successful participation in physical activities.

Critical thinkers find it satisfying to know when to say "no" to an idea or opinion and to know why that response is appropriate. If you regularly use the panning-for-gold approach, then anything that gets into your head will have been systematically examined first. When an idea or belief *does* pass the criteria developed here, it will make sense to agree with it—at least until new evidence appears.

The Importance of Practice

Our goal is to make your learning as simple as possible. However, the habit of critical thinking will initially take a lot of practice.

The practice exercises and sample responses at the end of each chapter, except this introductory chapter, are an important part of this text. Our answers are not necessarily the only correct ones, but they do provide illustrations of how to apply the definitions and question-asking skills. We intentionally failed to provide sample answers for the third passage at the end of each chapter. Our objective is to give you the opportunity to struggle with the answer using your knowledge of the chapter we have just studied. For additional practice opportunities and for online help, go to http://www.pearsonhighered.com/browne, where we have placed many helpful hints and practice materials.

THE RIGHT QUESTIONS

Just asking whatever questions pop into our mind is not very helpful. We need to be selective as Agent Brown in *The Matrix* reminded us, "Perhaps we are asking the wrong questions."

To give you an initial sense of the skills that *Asking the Right Questions* will help you acquire, we will list the critical questions for you here. By the time you reach the end of this book, you should know when and how to ask these questions effectively:

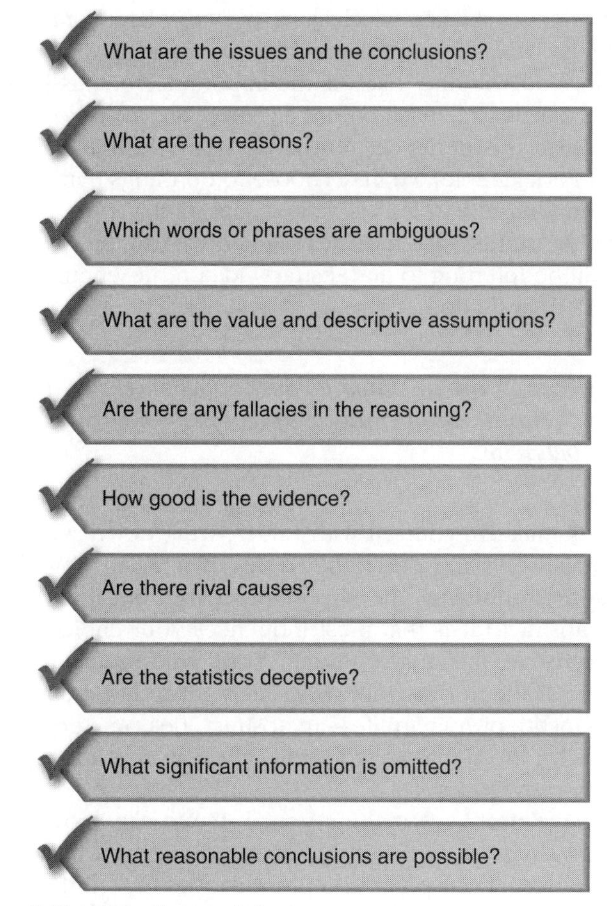

Critical Questions to Ask

CRITICAL THINKING IS A SOCIAL ACTIVITY

Much of our thinking is not a solo activity; it involves other people. We move forward by interacting attentively with other people; without them, we are lost as learners. Critical thinking relies heavily on being able to listen with respect to what others have to say.

Values and Other People

Think of other people as your most valuable resource, the basis for the facts, opinions, and conclusions that you will eventually have. In an important and ongoing manner, other people are part of your extended family, those who nurture your conclusions. The theme here is connectedness.

How these interactions work is shaped by your values and the values you perceive in those with whom you interact. Before you can discover the importance of values in shaping conclusions, you must have some understanding of what a value is. *Values*, as we will use the term, are ideas that someone thinks are worthwhile. You will find that it is the importance one assigns to *abstract ideas* that has the major influence on one's choices and behavior.

Usually objects, experiences, and actions are desired because of some idea we value. For example, we may choose to do things that provide us with contacts with important people. We value "important people" (concrete idea) because we value "status" (abstract idea). When we use the word *value* in this chapter, we will be referring to an (abstract) idea representing what someone thinks is important and good.

***Attention:** Values are unstated ideas that people see as worthwhile. They provide standards of conduct by which we measure the quality of human behavior.*

To better familiarize yourself with values, write down some of your own values. Try to avoid writing down the names of people, tangible objects, or actions. Pizza and tennis may be important to you, but it is the importance you assign to abstract ideas that most influences your choices and behavior concerning controversial public issues. Your willingness to argue for or against assisted suicide, for instance, is strongly related to the importance you assign to the sanctity of human life—an abstract idea. As you create your list of values, focus on those that are so significant that they affect your opinions and behavior in many ways.

Do you have problems making your list? We can provide some help. Values are *standards of conduct* that we endorse and expect people to meet. When we expect our political representatives to "tell the truth," we are indicating to them and to ourselves that honesty is one of our most cherished values. Ask yourself how you expect your friends to be. What standards of conduct would you want your children to develop? Answers to these questions should help you enlarge your understanding of values.

Let's remind ourselves how knowledge about values relates to the social nature of critical thinking. While we must require ourselves to listen carefully to those who have different value priorities than our own, the most obvious social link established by values is similarity. Those of us who see individual responsibility as an extremely important value tend to be comfortable with and to seek out those who similarly believe that *improved personal choices* are the solution to most human problems. Hence, many of our most valuable social interactions or learning experiences start with communications with those who have similar value priorities. Our huge challenge in this regard is to make ourselves work hard to understand the reasoning of those whose value priorities *differ* from ours.

While adventure, ambition, autonomy, comfort, excellence, justice, rationality, tolerance, and spontaneity may be important values to us, it is quite likely that other reasonable people will have important values that conflict with many of these. Our normal tendency to listen to only those with similar value priorities needs our active resistance. We have to fight against the tendency.

Primary Values of a Critical Thinker

This book is dedicated to help you become a critical thinker. As a critical thinker, you will be pursuing *better* conclusions, *better* beliefs, and *better* decisions. Certain values advance your effort to do so; others do not. By knowing and appreciating the primary values of a critical thinker, you have some mental muscle that you can use to remind yourself of the necessity of your paying close attention to those who do not share your value priorities. Let's examine these primary values.

1. Autonomy. At first this value may seem as if it has little to do with encouraging people to pay attention to those with different perspectives. How does a drive to form one's own conclusions encourage us in any fashion to seek and listen to views that are not our own? Aha! And what raw material should you use in pursuing this autonomy? Surely, we all want to pick and choose from the widest possible array of possibilities; otherwise, we may miss the one decision or option that we *would have chosen* if only we had paid attention to those who did not share our value priorities. For example, Democrats make a huge mistake if they listen only to other Democrats.
2. Curiosity. To take advantage of the panning-for-gold method of living your life, you need to listen and read, **really** listen and read. Other people have the power to move you forward, to liberate you from your current condition of partial knowledge. To be a critical thinker requires you to then ask questions about what you have encountered. Part of what you gain from other people is their insights and understanding, **when what they have to offer meets the standards of good reasoning** that you will learn in *Asking the Right Questions*.
3. Humility. Recognizing that even the smartest person in the world makes many mistakes each week provides the ideal platform for engaging actively with other people. Certainly some of us have insights that others do not have, but each of us is very limited in what we can do, and at honest moments, we echo Socrates when he said that he knew that he did not know. Once we accept this reality, we can better recognize that our experiences with other people can fill in at least a few of the gaps in our present understanding. Also, a sense of humility keeps us from avoiding a very common obstacle to critical thinking, the belief that "those who disagree with me are biased, but I am not."
4. Respect for good reasoning wherever you find it. While we want to respect and listen to other voices, all conclusions or opinions are not equally

worthwhile. The critical questions you will learn as you study this book will provide a framework to assist you in picking and choosing from among all the people trying to influence you. When you find strong reasoning, regardless of the race, age, political party, wealth, or citizenship of the speaker or writer, rely on it until a better set of reasoning comes along.

By all means, act with confidence based on your beliefs, but hold your conclusions with only that degree of firmness that permits you to still wonder to yourself, "Might I be wrong?"

THINKING AND FEELINGS

Making a list of the primary values of a critical thinker and describing them are relatively easy. But living those values is extraordinarily difficult. When you first encounter a conclusion, you do so with a history. You have learned to care about certain things, to support particular interests, and to discount claims of a particular type. So you always start to think critically in the midst of existing opinions. You have emotional commitments to these existing opinions.

They are *your* opinions, and you quite understandably feel protective of them. Listen as political satirist Stephen Colbert mocks this attitude of ours: "I'm not a fan of facts. You see, the facts can change, but my opinion will never change, no matter what the facts are."

When you change your mind, it almost seems as if you are admitting that you have been a gigantic failure until this moment. Having the courage to change your mind in the face of stronger reasoning that points you in a new direction requires superior dedication to creating the very best version of yourself that can be created. There is certainly no wisdom in changing your mind all the time just to show you are flexible. But when you encounter new evidence and fresh reasons that you can see are better than what you had been relying on, you owe it to yourself to move forward. You want to embrace this modified picture of your world, confident that it is more reliable. Flip-flopping for the right reasons is preferable to stubbornly holding on to conclusions based on poorly informed reasoning.

Keep in mind that when we are thinking, we have a purpose. In other words, we think to achieve something. When our thinking is motivated by a desire to keep heading in the same direction as our previous thinking, we are not reflecting the values of a critical thinker. Instead, we are an advocate, searching for better ways to protect the views we currently hold. From this perspective, to think is to defend.

The brighter, more growth-oriented alternative is to think so that we can achieve more depth and better accuracy. To achieve that purpose, we have to train ourselves to listen to the arguments of those with whom we disagree. We are already familiar with our own arguments; we stand to learn the most by familiarizing with those other arguments, the ones we really have not explored very thoroughly.

This point deserves special emphasis. We bring lots of personal baggage to every decision we make—experiences, dreams, values, training, and cultural habits. However, if you are to grow, you need to recognize these feelings, and, as much as you are able, put them on a shelf for a bit. Doing so is a constant struggle as Matchbox Twenty notes in their song, "Argue."

And I don't know, said I don't know
All these feelings, cloud up my reasoning
Cloud up my reasoning.

Only by trying to be aware of these feelings and their effects on you will you be able to listen carefully when others offer arguments that threaten or violate your current beliefs. This openness is important because many of our own positions on some issues are not especially reasonable ones; they are opinions given to us by others, and over many years, we develop emotional attachments to them. Indeed, we frequently believe that we are being personally attacked when someone presents a conclusion contrary to our own. The danger of being emotionally involved in an issue is that you may fail to consider potential good reasons for other positions—reasons that might be sufficient to change your mind on the issue if only you would listen to them.

Remember: Emotional involvement should not be the primary basis for accepting or rejecting a position. Ideally, emotional involvement should be most intense *after* reasoning has occurred. Critical thinkers, however, are not machines. They care greatly about many issues. The depth of that concern can be seen in their willingness to do all the hard mental work associated with critical thinking. But any passion felt by critical thinkers is moderated by the recognition that their current beliefs are open to revision.

KEEPING THE CONVERSATION GOING

Because critical thinking is a social activity, we need to consider how other people are likely to react to us when we ask them questions about their beliefs and conclusions. As long as we are interacting with others who share the primary values of critical thinking, our questions will be received as evidence that we are a partner in the search for better answers to the questions we share. But that terrific opportunity to grow together is not going to be the only kind of social interaction you will have.

Many people are not eager to have their thinking questioned; often, they experience questioning as annoying and unfriendly. Some may wonder, "Why is she asking me all these challenging questions? Why does she not just agree with me?" Don't be surprised if someone reacts to your quest to learn more by asking you why you are being so mean. Many people are unaccustomed to situations where someone is so excited to know more about why a particular viewpoint is held.

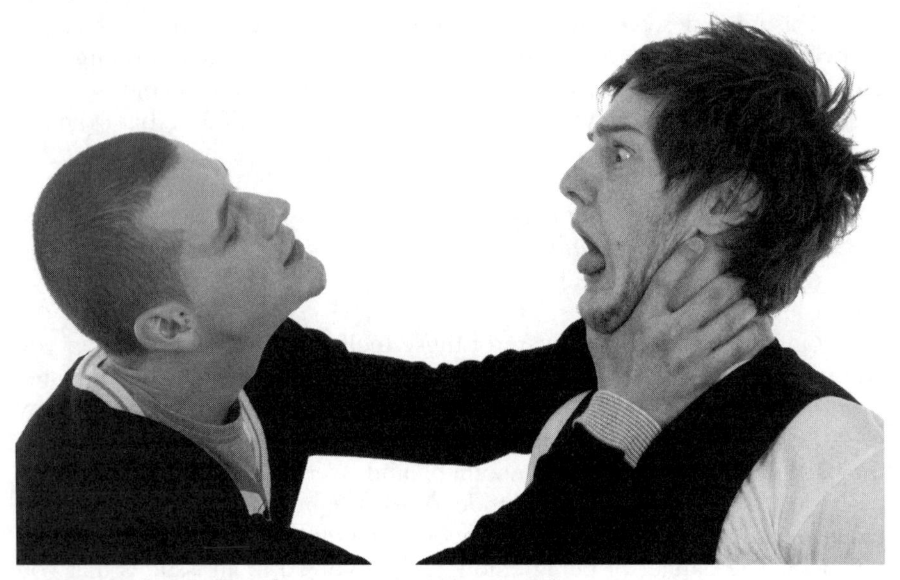

Common Understanding of an Argument © Shutterstock

For purposes of critical thinking, an argument is altogether something else. Because we see argument as the mechanism whereby we fertilize and prune our current conclusions, we will use the concept in a very different manner. An *argument* is a combination of two forms of statements: a conclusion and the reasons allegedly supporting it. The partnership between reasons and conclusion establishes a person's argument. It is something we provide because we care about how people live their lives and what they believe. Our continual improvement depends on someone's caring enough about us to offer us arguments and to evaluate the ones we make. Only then will we be able to develop as thoughtful people.

Above all else, when you use your critical thinking, make it clear to other people that you want to learn. Furthermore, give them assurances that you wish them well and that any disagreement you have with them, as serious and important as that disagreement might be, need not result in a verbal bloodbath. What follows are a few verbal strategies that you can use to keep the conversation going:

1. Try to clarify your understanding of what the other person intends by asking, "Did I hear you say?"
2. Ask the other person whether there is any evidence that would cause him to change his mind.
3. Suggest a time-out in which each of you will try to find the very best evidence for the conclusion you hold.
4. Ask why the person thinks the evidence on which you are relying is so weak.

5. Try to come together. If you take that person's best reasons and put them together with your best reasons, is there some conclusion that both of you could embrace?
6. Search for common values or other shared conclusions to serve as a basis for determining where the disagreement first appeared in your conversation.
7. Try to present a model of caring and calm curiosity; as soon as the verbal heat turns up, try to remind yourselves that you are learners, not warriors.
8. Make certain that your face and body suggest humility, rather than the demeanor of a know-it-all.

Creating a Friendly Environment for Communication

As a writer or speaker, you are faced with an important choice. You have to decide the type of environment you'll create for your audience. Will you choose one that is hostile to people who disagree with your conclusions? In the current polarized climate, the temptation is great. Just look at the tactics employed during the American election season—the tactics the *Daily Show*'s Jon Stewart mocked when he said, "I disagree with you, but I am pretty sure you're not Hitler."

In the spirit of this Jon Stewart quote, you could choose to create an environment in which reasonable people can productively and respectfully disagree—an environment that welcomes discussion and question-asking. Of course we prefer this approach, but let's be honest: There are some compelling reasons to write in a tone that excludes, even shoots down, critical thinkers.

First, it's easier to shoot down a hard question than to consider and respond to it. Plus, you'll surely sound authoritative, daring your audience to challenge your expert judgment. Not to mention that this writing style can even be fun. Have you ever read and enjoyed a vicious review of a movie, book, album, or video game?

Take a look at the tone and word choice in this review of the 2009 box office success *Transformers: Revenge of the Fallen*. Popular film critic Roger Ebert suggested:

> If you want to save yourself the ticket price, go into the kitchen, cue up a male choir singing the music of hell, and get a kid to start banging pots and pans together. Then close your eyes and use your imagination.

Just try to convince him that he should calm down and reconsider.

For communicators committed to critical thinking, the cost of this tone is too high. Imitating the approach of Ebert cuts us off from the thoughts of those we are trying to communicate with. They shut down conversation. In addition, this method directly conflicts with the values of a critical thinker, namely curiosity, humility, and respect for good reasoning. Arguing your position with the ferocity and conviction displayed by Ebert closes you off to that important critical thinking question: "Might I be wrong?" We want to encourage you to make your writing a hospitable place for readers who are different from you.

WISHFUL THINKING: PERHAPS THE BIGGEST SINGLE OBSTACLE TO CRITICAL THINKING

In 2005, Stephen Colbert reminded us of the dangerous mental habit of *truthiness*. A person is loyal to truthiness when he prefers concepts or facts he wishes to be true, rather than concepts or facts known to be true. We wish for the world to have such characteristics. Things would be much more fair and kind and productive. But in place of wondering about whether such a world is even close to reality, many of us just form beliefs to match our make-believe world. What we wish to be true, we simply declare *is* true. We want the product label to be honest and straightforward. So we buy with little hesitation believing that the product is precisely reflecting the words on the label.

That way, the facts conform to our beliefs rather than fitting our beliefs to the facts. We are sure you can see the problem here. Because we think that things should be different than they are, we believe that indeed they are different. Once we recognize this tendency in ourselves, we need to keep asking, "Is that true because I want it to be true, or is there convincing evidence that it's true?" Otherwise we will embarrass ourselves by saying something like Harry Potter says in *Harry Potter and the Half-Blood Prince*:

> Harry: It was Malfoy.
>
> Professor Minerva McGonagall: That is a very serious accusation, Potter.
>
> Professor Severus Snape: Indeed. Your evidence?
>
> Harry: I just know.
>
> Severus Snape: You...just...know? (sarcastically) Once again, you astound me with your gifts, Potter.

Wishful thinking has staying power because of the frequency of our denial patterns. Quite unconsciously, we fight with the facts, trying to reinforce visions of the world that are rosy beyond the bounds of reality. Anxieties and fears about the problems we face together and individually serve as a protective shield against seeing the actual world in which we live. Think of how frequently over the course of your life you will hear leaders of nations declare that the war they are fighting will soon be over, and victory will be won. But such predictions usually turn out to be hollow promises. To have to face the facts that the war may go on and on or that it will not result in a clear victory for the home team is just too painful to consider. So the mind erases it.

A form of wishful thinking is magical thinking. People tend to rely on magic as a causal explanation for explaining things that science has not acceptably explained, or to attempt to control things that science cannot. Listen as Bart Simpson deflates magical thinking:

> Marge: Alright kids, hand me your letters. I'll send them to Santa's workshop up at the North Pole.
>
> Bart: Oh, please. There's only one fat guy who brings us presents and his name ain't Santa.

Much of the world is beyond our control and we know we are up against forces and dilemmas that seem to exceed our reach to solve. We react by replacing the tooth fairy and the Easter bunny with some new source of alleged power and influence who can bring optimism and security to our thoughts. Magical thinking tends to be greatest when people feel most powerless to understand or alter a situation. In the face of great need, any belief in the randomness or accidental aspects of life is set aside as grim and replaced with the promise of magical causal relationships.

The antidote to wishful thinking is active use of the critical questions taught in this book. Obstacles to critical thinking will always be part of us; we cannot ignore them, but we can surely resist them with curiosity and a deep respect for the principles of critical thinking.

CHAPTER

What Are the Issue and the Conclusion?

Before we evaluate someone's reasoning, we must first find it. Doing so sounds simple; it isn't. To get started as a critical thinker, you must practice the identification of the issue and the conclusion.

> Cell phones are becoming a large part of today's society, bringing with them benefits and drawbacks. They are beneficial for those with tight schedules and in case of emergencies. Cell phones can also come in handy for parents to check up on their children. Even though cell phones do carry benefits, the drawbacks are in their inappropriate use. When a cell phone rings during a lecture or a concert, a major disruption in the concentration of others is inevitable. Even though there are suggestions in polite society to leave them off, perhaps we need stronger penalties associated with abuse of the growing population of cell phones.

The person who wrote this assessment of cell phones very much wants you to believe something. But what is that something and why are we supposed to believe any such thing?

In general, those who create Web pages, blogs, editorials, books, magazine articles, or speeches are trying to change your perceptions or beliefs. For you to form a reasonable reaction to their persuasive effort, you must first identify the controversy or *issue* as well as the thesis or conclusion being pushed onto you. (Someone's *conclusion* is her intended message to you. Its purpose is to shape your beliefs and/or behavior.) Fail to identify the author's conclusion, and you will be reacting to a distorted version of the attempted communication.

When you have completed this chapter, you should be able to answer the first of our critical questions successfully:

 *Critical Question:* ***What are the issue and the conclusion?***

Attention: *An issue is a question or controversy responsible for the conversation or discussion. It is the stimulus for what is being said.*

KINDS OF ISSUES

It will be helpful at this point to identify two kinds of issues you will typically encounter. The following questions illustrate one of these:

Does musical training improve a person's ability to learn math?

What is the most common cause of domestic abuse?

Is Paxil an effective way to treat depression?

How much will health care cost in 2016 in the United States?

How good is the psychology graduate school at the University of Illinois?

All these questions have one thing in common. They require answers attempting to describe the way the world was, is, or is going to be. For example, answers to the first two questions might be: "In general, children who are musically trained learn math more easily than nonmusical children," and "Chronic alcohol use is the most common cause of domestic abuse."

Such issues are *descriptive issues*. They are commonly found in textbooks, magazines, the Internet, and television. Such issues reflect our curiosity about patterns or order in the world. Note the boldfaced words that begin each question above; when questions begin with these words, they will probably be descriptive questions.

Attention: *Descriptive issues are those that raise questions about the accuracy of descriptions of the past, present, or future.*

Now let's look at examples of a second kind of question:

Should intelligent design be taught in the public schools?

What ought to be done about Medicaid fraud?

Must we outlaw SUVs or face increasing rates of asthma?

All of these questions require answers suggesting the way the world *ought to be*. For example, answers to the first two questions might be:

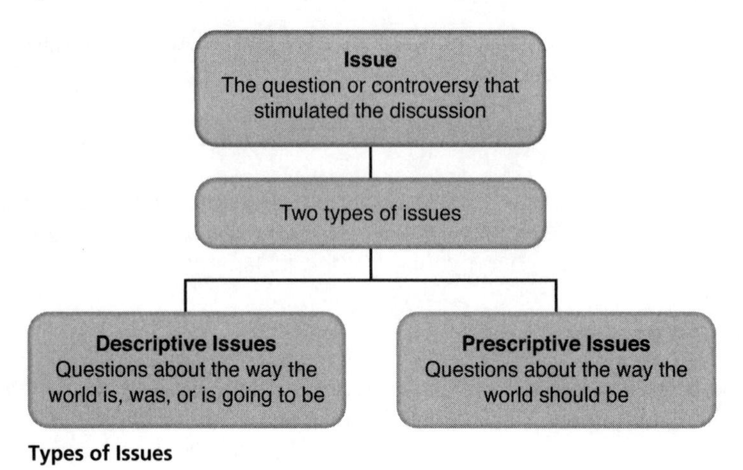

Types of Issues

"Intelligent design *should* be taught in the public schools," and "We *ought* to impose more severe penalties for Medicaid fraud."

These issues are ethical or moral; they raise questions about what is right or wrong, desirable or undesirable, good or bad. They demand prescriptive answers. Thus, we will refer to these issues as *prescriptive issues*. Social controversies are often prescriptive issues.

We have somewhat oversimplified. Sometimes, it will be difficult to decide what kind of issue is being discussed. Keeping these distinctions in mind, however, is useful because the kinds of critical evaluations you eventually make will differ depending on the kind of issue to which you are responding.

Attention:* *Prescriptive issues are those that raise questions about what we should do or what is right or wrong, good or bad.

SEARCHING FOR THE ISSUE

How does one go about determining the basic question or issue? Sometimes, it is very simple: The writer or speaker will tell you what it is. Alternatively, the issue may be identified in the body of the text, usually right at the beginning, or it may even be found in the title. When the issue is explicitly stated, it will be indicated by phrases such as the following:

The question I am raising is: Why must we have laws regulating tobacco products?

Lowering the legal drinking age: *Is it the right thing to do?*

Should sex education be taught in the schools?

Unfortunately, the question is not always explicitly stated and instead must be inferred from other clues in the communication. For example, many writers or speakers react to some current event that concerns them, such as a series of violent acts in schools. Asking "What is the author reacting to?" will often suggest the central issue of a communication. Another good clue is knowledge of the author's background, such as organizations to which she belongs. So check for background information about the author as you try to determine the issue.

When you are identifying the issue, try to resist the idea that there is one and only one correct way to state the issue. Once you have identified a question that the entire essay or speech is addressing, and the link between that question and the essay or speech, *you have found the issue.* Just make certain that what you are calling an issue meets the definitional criteria that define an "issue."

The surest way to detect an issue when it is not explicitly stated, however, is to locate the conclusion. In many cases, the conclusion must be found before you can identify the issue. Thus, in such cases, the first step in critical evaluation is to find the conclusion—a frequently difficult step.

WE CANNOT CRITICALLY EVALUATE UNTIL WE FIND THE CONCLUSION!

Let's see how we go about looking for that very important structural element.

***Attention:** A conclusion is the message that the speaker or writer wishes you to accept.*

SEARCHING FOR THE AUTHOR'S OR SPEAKER'S CONCLUSION

To identify the conclusion, the critical thinker must ask, "What is the writer or speaker trying to prove?" or "What is the communicator's main point?" The answer to either of these questions will be the conclusion. Also, any answer to the question provided by the speaker or writer will be the conclusion.

In searching for a conclusion, you will be looking for a statement or set of statements that the writer or speaker wants you to believe. She wants you to believe the conclusion on the basis of her other statements. In short, the basic structure of persuasive communication or argument is: *This* because of *that.* *This* refers to the conclusion; *that* refers to the support for the conclusion. This structure represents the process of *inference.*

Conclusions are *inferred*; they are derived from reasoning. Conclusions are ideas that require other ideas to support them. Thus, whenever someone claims something is true or ought to be done and provides no statements to support her claim, that claim is not a conclusion because that person has not offered any basis for belief. In contrast, unsupported claims are what we refer to as *mere* opinions.

Understanding the nature of a conclusion is an essential step toward critical reading and listening. Let's look closely at a conclusion and at the inference process. Here is a brief paragraph; see whether you can identify the conclusion, then the statements that support it.

> Factory farming should not be legal. There are other more natural ways to produce needed food supply.

"Factory farming should not be legal" is the author's answer to the question: Should factory farming be legalized? It is her conclusion. The author supports this belief with another reason: "There are other more natural ways to produce needed food supply."

Do you see why the supporting belief is not a conclusion? It is not the conclusion because it is used to prove something else. *Remember:* To believe *one statement* (the conclusion) because you think it is supported by *other* beliefs is to make an inference. When people engage in this process, they are reasoning; the conclusion is the outcome of this reasoning.

Sometimes, communicators will not make their conclusions explicit; in such cases, you will have to infer the conclusion from what you believe the author is trying to prove by the set of ideas she has presented.

USING THIS CRITICAL QUESTION

Once you have found the conclusion, use it as the focus of your evaluation. It is the destination that the writer or speaker wants you to choose. Your ongoing concern is: Should I accept that conclusion on the basis of what is supporting the claim?

CLUES TO DISCOVERY: HOW TO FIND THE CONCLUSION

Clue No. 1: **Ask what the issue is.** Because a conclusion is always a response to an issue, it will help you find the conclusion if you know the issue. We discussed earlier how to identify the issue. First, look at the title. Next, look at the opening paragraphs. If this technique does not help, skimming several pages may be necessary.

Clue No. 2: **Look for indicator words.** The conclusion will frequently be preceded by indicator words that announce a conclusion is coming. When you see these indicator words, take note of them. They tell you that a conclusion may follow. A list of such indicator words follows:

consequently	suggests that
therefore	thus
it follows that	the point I'm trying to make is
shows that	proves that
indicates that	the truth of the matter is

Read the following passage; then identify and highlight the indicator words. By doing so, you will have identified the statements containing the conclusion.

> Because of the wording of the Constitution, it follows that prayer should not be allowed in public schools. When the schools favor any particular religion, they are hampering the freedom of those who embrace a different religion. The idea of freedom of religion is what the country was founded on.

You should have highlighted the following phrase: *it follows*. The conclusion follows these words.

Unfortunately, many written and spoken communications do not introduce the conclusion with indicator words. However, when *you* communicate with the goal of making your conclusion clear to your audience, you should draw attention to your thesis with indicator words. Those words act as a neon sign, drawing attention to the point you want the reader to accept.

Clue No. 3: **Look in likely locations.** Conclusions tend to occupy certain locations. The first two places to look are at the beginning and at the end. Many writers begin with a statement of purpose, containing what they are trying to prove. Others summarize their conclusions at the end. If you are reading a long, complex passage and are having difficulty seeing where it is going, skip ahead to the end.

Clue No. 4: **Remember what a conclusion is not.** Conclusions will not be any of the following:

- examples
- statistics
- definitions
- background information
- evidence

Clue No. 5: **Check the context of the communication and the author's background.** Often writers, speakers, or Internet sites take predictable positions on issues. Knowing probable biases of the source and the background of the authors can be especially valuable clues when the conclusion is not explicit. Be particularly alert to information about organizations with which writers or speakers may be associated.

Clue No. 6: **Ask the question, "and therefore?"** Because conclusions are often implied, ask for the identity of the "and therefore" element. Ask, "Does the author want us to draw an implied conclusion from the information communicated?" Conclusions like "candidate X will be soft on crime" are often left for the reader or viewer to infer from the limited information presented in a political advertisement.

CRITICAL THINKING AND YOUR OWN WRITING AND SPEAKING

Have you ever read one of your classmate's papers and wondered "so, um, what was the point?" Sure, you have a fuzzy idea that this classmate has an ax to grind with Ticketmaster's exorbitant fees, but a fuzzy idea is about all you have. When we write, we often think our meaning is crystal clear. After all, our argument seems perfectly clear to us. Unfortunately, several barriers keep our readers from easily understanding that which is transparent to us. Our readers cannot hear our inner thoughts and our many hidden beliefs. They do not know our values or backgrounds. They have no access to our research or our brainstorming notes. All they have is the page or screen in front of them. For this reason, we urge you to make a special effort to be clear and transparent in your writing. You should expect to hear this message from us again over the course of our writing suggestions. One of the greatest barriers to critical thinking is a failure to bridge the communication gap.

Narrowing Your Issue Prior to Writing

Since high school composition classes, you have probably been urged to take time to outline your thoughts before jumping into a writing assignment. You may have learned different prewriting techniques such as brainstorming, webbing, or free-writing. Maybe you take these suggestions very seriously, but for many of you, we suspect that jumping straight into a project is too great a temptation. You tend to just figure it out as you go.

Whether your prewriting approach is painstaking or more off the cuff, we urge you to take a moment to determine your issue prior to delving into your writing. One of the qualities that distinguishes mature writers from developing writers is the presence of a clear precise issue.

We encourage you to take the time to consider your issue prior to writing for another reason. Authors who do not do so often unknowingly bite off more than they can chew. In a three- to five-page writing assignment, for instance, a young writer may try to prove to his readers that climate change exists, what causes climate change, why critiques of climate change are wrong, *and* why the reader should be concerned. Each of these issues is interesting and important, but within the confines of the writing sample, this writer may have tried to do too much.

Cluing Your Reader into Your Conclusion

When you write, you want to leave your readers with absolutely no doubt about the argument through which you are trying to persuade them. Your conclusion and your reasons should be easily identifiable. When you are writing or speaking with the purpose of communicating a particular conclusion, your readers or listeners will be looking for it. Help them by giving it the clarity it deserves. It is the central message you want to deliver. Emphasize it; leave no doubt about what it actually is. Making your conclusion easily identifiable not only makes a reader's task easier, but may also improve the logic of your writing.

Our writing suggestions have an overarching theme: Writers, ourselves included, need to make a special effort to organize their thoughts and express them explicitly. While they may seem as clear as day to us, our readers do not have our intimate knowledge. If we make this effort, we will help bridge the communication gap between writers and readers and facilitate critical thinking discussion.

PRACTICE EXERCISES

? *Critical Question:* ***What are the issue and the conclusion?***

In the following passages, locate the issue and the conclusion. As you search, be sure to look for indicator words. Notice that a self-talk model of this critical thinking process follows the first passage. By thinking aloud about how we would approach this passage, we hope to make it easier for you to ask and answer the critical questions in the future. We provide a more condensed version of a sample response for passage 2 and leave you on your own to find the issue and conclusion for the third practice passage.

Passage 1

Homeschooling is a valid concept if the parent makes teaching a full-time job and has the insight, knowledge, and patience to do so. However, the truth of the matter is that it is usually a mistake for parents to homeschool their child.

Parents may choose to pull their student out of public schools for the wrong reasons. Sometimes, when children have a discipline problem, the parents will pull them out of school rather than tolerating the rules associated with the punishment. Such a motivation does not speak well for the probable results of the homeschooling that follows. In addition, when there are no other adults to monitor what is going on at home, it is likely that if there is a case of abuse in the home, it will go unnoticed. Society needs to know whether these children are getting the education and treatment they deserve.

Passage 2

Television advertising agencies are very clever in the way that they construct ads. Often, the ads are similar to the cartoons that children enjoy. Children see these characters interacting with a certain product and associate their affection for the character with affection for the product. The companies do not want children to perceive a difference between the shows they are watching and the advertisements. By using this strategy, these companies take advantage of the fact that children are often not able to discriminate between the cartoons and the ads and do not understand that the things offered come at a cost. Often, the advertising is about sugary snacks or fatty foods, leading children down a path to bad health. Advertising geared toward children should be regulated—just as there are regulations now about tobacco and alcohol ads targeted at children.

Passage 3

Should the public be shown actual courtroom trials on television? It seems as though the system can easily be corrupted by having cameras in the courtroom. Victims are hesitant enough when testifying in front of a small crowd, but their knowledge that every word is being sent to countless homes would increase the likelihood that they would simply refuse to testify. There is little to no assumed innocence for the accused when their trial is shown on television. People do not watch court television because they are concerned about our country's ability to effectively carry out the proceedings of the judicial system; instead, they are looking for the drama in witness testimony: entertainment. Thus, leave the cameras out of the courtrooms, and let the public view sitcom drama based on the legal system.

Sample Responses

Passage 1

- *Sometimes, the issue is easy to find because it's explicitly stated in an argument. I don't think that this argument explicitly mentions the issue because the author never mentions the question that sparked the argument. My next move should be to find the conclusion. Then I'll be able to more easily find the issue. Asking the Right Questions said that the surest way to find an issue that is not explicitly mentioned in the text is to find the conclusion.*

- *Looking for indicator words may help me find the conclusion. "The truth of the matter" was listed as an indication of a conclusion and is used in the argument. Maybe the conclusion is, "It is usually a mistake for parents to home-school their child." This statement really could be the conclusion. Another suggestion for finding the conclusion was to look in the introduction and conclusion. And the sentence is in the introduction.*
- *Asking the Right Questions provided me with a list of components of arguments that are not the conclusion. I should check to make sure that the statement "Few parents who home-school their child are capable of doing so" is not a statistic, an example, a definition, background information, or other evidence. Clearly, it is not.*
- *At this point, I am mostly certain that the conclusion is that "It is usually a mistake for parents to home-school their child. The indicator words suggested it, the location confirmed this belief, and it did not fall into the list of components of arguments sometimes mistaken for the conclusion.*
- *Next, I need to figure out what question stimulated this discussion, or the issue. If the conclusion is that "It is usually a mistake for parents to home-school their child," the issue that stimulated this discussion might be, "Is it desirable for parents to homeschool their child?" This issue can be inferred from the conclusion, and all the subsequent sentences that discuss potential problems with homeschooling.*
- *Before I conclude, I want to figure out whether this issue is prescriptive or descriptive. To do so, I need to ask myself whether the author is describing a situation or prescribing a position about right and wrong, desirable and undesirable, good and bad. The author details some problems with homeschooling and suggests that society needs to know that these children are receiving "the education and treatment that they deserve." These statements raise questions about whether a situation—homeschooling—is desirable. The issue, therefore, must be a prescriptive issue.*

Passage 2

There are no indicator words to point toward the conclusion, but a good place to look for the conclusion is at either the beginning or the end of the excerpt. In this case, the very last statement is the conclusion, and you can tell it is the conclusion because it gives finality to the passage using the phrase "should be." This phrase also indicates that this is a prescriptive issue. It is not talking about the way things are or are not, but how they ought to be. The issue is assumed from the conclusion and from the preceding statements explaining why the author came to her conclusion.

ISSUE: *Should advertisements geared toward children be regulated?*
CONCLUSION: *Advertisements geared toward children should be regulated.*

CHAPTER 3

What Are the Reasons?

Reasons provide answers for our human curiosity about why someone makes a particular decision or holds a particular opinion. Consider the following statements:

1. The government should protect only a select number of endangered species from extinction.
2. A centipede sting is more dangerous than the bite of most snakes.
3. Schools should have the right to search students' lockers for drugs and weapons.

Those three claims are each missing something. We may or may not agree with them, but in their current form, they are neither weak nor strong. None of the claims contains an explanation or rationale for *why* we should agree. Thus, if we heard someone make one of those three assertions, we would be left hungry for more.

What is missing is the reason or reasons responsible for the claims. *Reasons* are beliefs, evidence, metaphors, analogies, and other statements offered to support or justify conclusions. They are the statements that form the basis for creating the credibility of a conclusion. Chapter 2 gave you some guidelines for locating two very important parts of the structure of an argument—the issue and the conclusion. This chapter focuses on techniques for identifying the third essential element of an argument—the reasons.

When a writer has a conclusion she wants you to accept, she must present reasons to persuade you that she is right and to show you *why*.

It is the mark of a rational person to support her beliefs with adequate proof, especially when the beliefs are of a controversial nature. For example, when someone asserts that China will soon overtake the United States as the dominant country in the world, this assertion should be met with the challenge, "Why do you say such a thing?" The person's reasons may be either strong or weak, but you will not know until you have asked the question and identified the reasons. If the answer is "because I think so," you should be dissatisfied with the argument because the "reason" is a mere restatement of the conclusion. However, if the answer is evidence concerning the projected military and educational expenditures of the two countries, you will want to consider such evidence when you evaluate the conclusion. *Remember:* ***You cannot determine the worth of a conclusion until you identify the reasons.***

Identifying reasons is an essential step in critical thinking. An opinion cannot be evaluated fairly unless we ask why it is held and receive a satisfactory response. Focusing on reasons requires us to remain open to and tolerant of views that might differ from our own. If we reacted to conclusions rather than to reasoning, we would tend to stick to the conclusions we brought to the discussion or essay, and those conclusions that agree with our own would receive our rapid agreement. If we are ever to reexamine our own opinions, we must remain curious, open to the reasons provided by those people with opinions that we do not yet share.

Critical Question: ***What are the reasons?***

The combination of the reasons and the conclusion results in what we defined in Chapter 2 as the "argument".

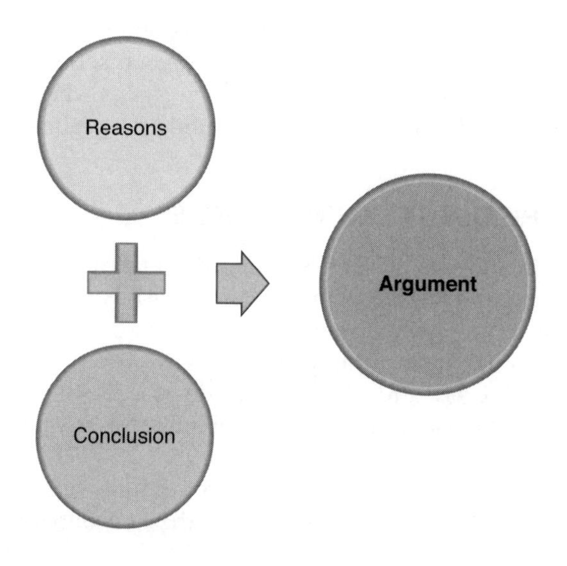

Sometimes, an argument will consist of a single reason and a conclusion; often, however, several reasons will be offered to support the conclusion. So when we refer to someone's argument, we might be referring to a single reason and its related conclusion or to the entire group of reasons and the conclusion it is intended to substantiate.

***Attention:** Reasons are explanations or rationales for why we should believe a particular conclusion.*

As we use the terms, *argument* and *reasoning* mean the same thing—the use of one or more ideas to support another idea. Thus, when a communication lacks reasons, it is neither an argument nor an example of reasoning. Consequently, only arguments and reasoning can be logically flawed. Because a reason *by itself* is an isolated idea, it cannot reflect a logical relationship.

Several characteristics of arguments grab our attention:

- They have intent. Those who provide arguments hope to convince us to believe certain things or to act in certain ways. Consequently, they call for a reaction. We can imitate the sponge or the gold prospector, but we ordinarily must respond somehow.
- Their quality varies. Critical thinking is required to determine the extent of quality in an argument.
- They have two essential visible components—a conclusion and reasons. Failure to identify either component destroys the opportunity to evaluate the argument. We cannot evaluate what we cannot identify.

That last point deserves some repetition and explanation. There is little purpose in rushing critical thinking. In fact, the philosopher Wittgenstein suggests that when one bright person addresses another, each should first say "Wait!" Taking the time to locate arguments before we assess what we think might have been said is only fair to the person providing the argument.

INITIATING THE QUESTIONING PROCESS

The first step in identifying reasons is to approach the argument with a questioning attitude, and the first question you should ask is *why*. You have identified the conclusion; now you wish to know why the conclusion makes sense. If a statement does not answer the question, "Why does the writer or speaker believe that?" then it is not a reason. To function as a reason, a statement (or a group of statements) must be used by a communicator as support or grounds for a conclusion.

Let us apply the questioning attitude to the following paragraph. First we will find the conclusion; then we will ask the appropriate *why* question.

Remember your guidelines for finding the conclusion. (The indicator words for the conclusion have been italicized.)

> (1) Should pilots be required to carry pepper spray? (2) Pilots were surveyed about their opinions. (3) Many indicated that they never know what to expect from their passengers, and they thought that pepper spray would help ensure passenger safety. (4) Fifty-seven percent of the pilots agreed that pepper spray would increase safety. (5) Therefore, airlines should require their pilots to carry pepper spray.

What follows *"Therefore"* answers the question raised in statement (1). Thus, the conclusion is statement (5) ". . . airlines should require their pilots to carry pepper spray." *Highlight the conclusion!*

Attention:* *An argument consists of a conclusion and the reasons that allegedly support it.

We then ask the question, "Why does the writer or speaker believe the conclusion?" The statements that answer that question are the reasons. In this particular case, the writer provides us with survey evidence as reasons. Statements (3) and (4) jointly provide the evidence; that is, together they provide support for the conclusion, thus serving as the reason for it. Thus, we can paraphrase the reason as follows: A majority of the surveyed pilots believe that pepper spray would enhance the safety of passengers.

Now, try to find the reasons in the following paragraph. Again, first find the conclusion, highlight it, and then ask the *why* question.

> (1) Genetic screening of embryos should not be allowed. (2) People do not have the right to play God and terminate a potential life just because it might not be the right sex or may have a defect of some kind. (3) I've had two autistic children and they are both happy. (4) It cannot be said that a person's quality of life is severely changed by birth defect.

The indicator word *should* in the first sentence signals the conclusion: The author is against genetic screening of embryos. Why does the author believe this? The main reason given is "People don't have the right to play God and decide to terminate a potential life based on a set of their preferred criteria." Sentences (3) and (4) together provide an additional reason for the author's belief: Personal positive experience with autistic children demonstrates that a person's quality of life is not severely changed by a birth defect.

As you determine a communicator's reasoning structure, you should treat any idea that seems to be used to support her conclusion as a reason, even if you do not believe that it actually provides support for the conclusion. At this stage of critical thinking, you are trying to identify the argument. Because you want to be fair to the person who made the argument, you want to use the principle of charity. If the writer or speaker believes she is providing support for the conclusion with some evidence or logic, then we should at least consider the reasoning. There will be plenty of time later to evaluate the reasoning carefully.

WORDS THAT IDENTIFY REASONS

As was the case with conclusions, certain words will typically indicate that a reason will follow. *Remember:* The structure of reasoning is *this, because of that.* Thus, the word *because,* as well as words synonymous with and similar in function to it, will frequently signal the presence of reasons. A list of indicator words for reasons follows:

as a result of	for the reason that
because of the fact that	in view of
is supported by	because the evidence is
studies show	first . . . second . . . third

KINDS OF REASONS

There are many different kinds of reasons, depending on the kind of issue. Many reasons will be statements that present evidence. By *evidence,* we mean specific information that someone uses to furnish proof for something she is trying to claim is true. Communicators appeal to many kinds of evidence to prove their point. These include the facts, research findings, examples from real life, statistics, appeals to experts and authorities, personal testimonials, and analogies. Different kinds of evidence are more appropriate in some situations than in others, and you will find it helpful to develop rules for yourself for determining what kinds of evidence are appropriate on given occasions.

You will often want to ask, "What kind of evidence is needed to support this claim?" and then determine whether such evidence has been offered. You should know that there are no uniform "codes of evidence" applicable to all cases of serious reasoning. A more detailed treatment of evidence appears in Chapters 7 and 8.

When a speaker or writer is trying to support a descriptive conclusion, the answer to the *why* question will typically be the evidence.

The following example provides a descriptive argument; try to find the author's reasons.

> The number of illegal immigrants in the United States is falling sharply. Studies indicate that their number fell by nearly 1 million people from 2008 to 2009.

You should have identified the first statement as the conclusion. It is a descriptive statement about the decreasing number of illegal immigrants. The rest of the paragraph presents the evidence—the reason for the conclusion. *Remember:* The conclusion itself will not be evidence; it will be a belief supported by evidence or by other beliefs.

In prescriptive arguments, reasons are typically either general, prescriptive statements or descriptive beliefs or principles. The use of these kinds of statements to support a conclusion in a prescriptive argument is illustrated in the following:

> (1) In today's society, there are all sorts of regulations on media, such as television ratings. (2) Do these ratings allow for people to make educated decisions about what they will or will not watch? (3) Do these ratings entice some people to watch a show even though they know they are not supposed to? (4) How many parents actually go by the television ratings to deter their children from watching a show? (5) More often than not, the television ratings do not prevent children from watching shows that society believes they are not mature enough to watch. (6) Television ratings are unenforceable guidelines. (7) If one believes in the censorship of media for minors, items such as the V-chip should be used for this purpose rather than the simple tagged rating at the top of the screen.

The conflict here is about whether television ratings are desirable. The author argues that if society really is concerned about what children are watching, then it should implement the use of items such as the V-chip, as stated in sentence (7). Let us look for sentences that answer the question, "Why does the author believe this conclusion?" First, note that no evidence is presented. Sentences (2) and (3) jointly form one reason, a descriptive belief: The television ratings are not significant enough to affect change, and they may even encourage some to watch more harmful shows than they would have otherwise watched. The warnings are vague and can leave people thinking that the show may not be that "bad."

Sentences (4) and (5) add a second reason: The television ratings do not really affect the choice of television shows for either parents or children. Sentence (6) provides a third reason: Television ratings cannot be enforced. These last two reasons are general beliefs. If the argument were expanded by the author, the beliefs themselves might be supported by evidence in some form.

KEEPING THE REASONS AND CONCLUSIONS STRAIGHT

Much reasoning is long and not very well organized. Sometimes, a set of reasons will support one conclusion, and that conclusion will function as the main reason for another conclusion. Reasons may be supported by other reasons. In complicated arguments, it is frequently difficult to keep the structure straight in your mind as you attempt to critically evaluate what you have read. To overcome this problem, try to develop your own organizing procedure for keeping the reasons and conclusions separate and in a logical pattern.

We have mentioned a number of techniques for you to use in developing a clear picture of the reasoning structure. If some other technique works better for you, by all means use it. The important point is to keep the reasons and conclusions straight as you prepare to evaluate.

Clues for Identifying and Organizing the Reasoning of a Passage

1. Circle indicator words.
2. Underline the reasons and conclusion in different colors of ink, or highlight the conclusion and underline the reasons.
3. Label the reasons and conclusion in the margin.
4. After reading long passages, make a list of reasons at the end of the essay.

USING THIS CRITICAL QUESTION

Once you have found the reasons, you need to come back to them again and again as you read or listen further. The conclusion depends on the merit of the reasons. *Weak reasons create weak reasoning!*

Reasons First, Then Conclusions

The first chapter warned you about the danger of weak-sense critical thinking. A warning signal that can alert you to weak-sense critical thinking should go off when you notice that reasons seem to be created (on the spot, even) only because they defend a previously held opinion. When someone is eager to share an opinion as if it were a conclusion but looks puzzled or angry when asked for reasons, weak-sense critical thinking is the probable culprit.

Certainly, you have a large set of initial beliefs, which act as initial conclusions when you encounter controversies. As your respect for the importance of reasons grows, you will frequently expect those conclusions to stand or crumble on the basis of their support. Your strongest conclusions follow your reflection about the reasons and what they mean.

Be your own censor in this regard. You must shake your own pan when looking for gold. Try to avoid "reverse logic" or "backward reasoning," whereby reasons are an afterthought, following the selection of your conclusion. Ideally, reasons are the tool by which conclusions are shaped and modified.

CRITICAL THINKING AND YOUR OWN WRITING AND SPEAKING

Your reasoning is arguably the most important aspect of your academic writing. Outlining and defending your reasons often take up a sizable portion of your writing. The quality of your reasons largely determines whether you persuade your readers. Because of its particular importance, writers need to be particularly attentive to their reasons at both the prewriting and writing stage. To do so, we encourage you to consider the following suggestions.

Exploring Possible Reasons before Reaching a Conclusion

Earlier in this chapter, we discouraged you from employing "reverse logic" or "backward reasoning." A writer concerned with critical thinking, instead, considers and weighs possible reasons and then comes to a conclusion.

The amount of initial research you will conduct before starting a writing project varies. In some instances, you will decide on an issue for a writing project that will require you to start from scratch with your research. For instance, you may have encountered a brief mention of modern dancer and choreographer Alvin Ailey in a reading for your introductory fine arts class. It sparked your interest, and you decided to take advantage of the writing project to learn more. In other circumstances, you will start a research project with some background knowledge. You may even select a project because you have had a lifetime interest in it. You have an ongoing passion for the original *Star Wars*, for example, and decided to use that interest as a springboard for a project.

Perhaps you are already a budding expert in *Star Wars*, American Roller Derby, or cyberpunk literature. It may be tempting to think you do not need to conduct more research. We hope we can convince you to reconsider. Even if you have conducted research in the past, you should still explore other possible reasons. For one, your previous research may have occurred before you decided to adopt the standards of a critical thinker. It may have been one sided. More likely, you may have conducted the research informally, without making a concerted effort to explore a breadth of reasons and evidence. Another reason why you should still explore other possible reasons is that your previous research may not be the most up to date.

In the 21st century, often a writer's first step toward exploring potential reasons is to head to Google or some other general search engine. While an incredibly valuable resource, when a search engine provides you with 424,000 results (the Google result for Alvin Ailey) or 6,050,000 results (the results for Cyberpunk in Google), it's clear that general search engines are often too extensive and broad to be very useful. We'd like to offer a couple of suggestions so that your search does not end there.

Identify Major Publications That Cover Your Issue

If your issue explores a political or social subject in current events, such as public education reform or the War on Terrorism, start with major news publications. The *New York Times*, *Washington Post*, *Wall Street Journal*, and *USA Today* have the highest readership in the United States. University and public libraries hold subscriptions to them. Academic databases such as LexisNexis permit you to search and access articles from them and other major newspapers. Many newspapers provide free access to at least a portion of their articles on their Web sites, including the four we listed.

Nearly every field of interest has major publications, from music (*Rolling Stone*, *Pitchfork*, and *Spin*) to business (*Forbes*, *Fortune,* and the *Bloomberg Markets*). By taking the time to explore several major publications that cover your issue, you update yourself on the current discussion. You also immerse yourself in the debate, learning what issues other writers have found intriguing or controversial. You can also use the articles you uncover as a springboard for more research. For instance, let's say you were intrigued by the candidacy of Christine O'Donnell, the Tea Party candidate for the 2010 Senate election in Delaware. After reading that O'Donnell admitted to "dabbling in witchcraft" in her youth, you decided to explore the issue, "To what extent should a candidate's personal history influence voters?"

Helping Your Readers Identify Your Reasons

When you are writing or speaking, you will want to keep your audience foremost in your thoughts. They need to be clear about what you conclude and why you have come to that conclusion. Display your reasons openly.

Help out your reader find your reasons by employing indicator words and phrases within your sentences. Certain words send the signal "Here comes one of my reasons!" To aid you in identifying reasons in your reading, we gave you a list of some of these signal words earlier in the chapter.

Another way to help your reader identify your reasoning is to give them a blueprint. A blueprint is an outline or a sketch of what is to come. You can outline what is to come by concisely introducing your reasons early in your writing. Your readers will then know what to expect from you.

PRACTICE EXERCISES

? *Critical Question:* ***What are the reasons?***

First survey the passage and highlight its conclusion. Then ask the question, "Why?" and locate the reasons. Use indicator words to help. Keep the conclusions and the reasons separate. Try to paraphrase the reasons; putting them in your own words helps clarify their meaning and function.

Passage 1

Public swimming pools can be a health hazard. Many public pools are not able to follow the sanitation regulations and therefore allow for the contraction of waterborne bacteria. Studies have shown that 60 percent of public pools are not able to maintain the proper amount of chlorine in the water, allowing pool users to be infected. Many users have become ill after the use of a public swimming pool.

Passage 2

Schools all around the nation are forming community service programs. Should students be required to do community service? There are many drawbacks to requiring such service.

Students will not be able to understand the concept of charity and benevolence if it is something they have to do. Forced charity seems contradictory to the concept of charity. If this concept loses value for the students because the service was not a choice, they will then resent the idea of community service and not volunteer to do so at a later time in life.

Furthermore, because this community service would be coerced, the students may not perform at a high level. They may feel they will do the bare minimum of what is required. The students may also be resentful or rude to the people they are helping, which would also hamper the progress of the community service. As you can see, forced community service may not be the best programming choice for schools.

Passage 3

In high school, men's basketball and men's football usually dominate the Friday-night schedule. Should it be that way? These games are significant to the high school experience, but not at the cost of the other sports in the school. Just because it has been a tradition does not mean that the format has to remain that way.

It is easier for most parents and other fans to make it out to the game on Friday nights. Therefore, it is easier for them to come see the men's basketball or men's football games.

What about the girl's basketball team or the swim team? Their games should not always be stuck on weekday afternoons and evenings. Their families often are not able to make it out to see them because most parents are working during the afternoons. The students who play these "secondary" sports are not getting a fair share of the spotlight; the schedule should change to accommodate these other sports.

Sample Responses

Passage 1

ISSUE: *Are public pools a health hazard?*

CONCLUSION: *Yes, they are.*

REASONS: 1. Many schools are not able to obey sanitation regulations.

(SUPPORTING REASONS)

a. *Sixty percent of public pools are not able to maintain proper chlorination levels.*

b. Many people have gotten sick after using public pools.

Recall that we are looking for the support system for the conclusion. We ask ourselves: Why does this person claim that there is a health hazard in public pools? The descriptive conclusion is justified by two reasons: a survey finding and an assertion that many users have become ill. Indicator words for the supporting reason are "studies have shown."

Passage 2

ISSUE: *Should schools require community service?*

CONCLUSION: *No, schools should not require community service.*

REASONS: 1. Forced charity makes little sense.

(SUPPORTING REASONS)

a. *Required community service is a self-contradiction, which may cause resentment and resistance to further volunteer work.*

b. Because of coercion, students will not perform at a high level.

1. *The students will only do the bare minimum, not what would most benefit the recipient.*
2. *Students may be rude to those they are helping.*

Why are we told that schools should not require community service? The answer to that question will be the author's reasons. The first reason is supported by a collection of examples and claims, all showing us that forced community service is a contradiction. *Furthermore* is the indicator word calling our attention to the second supporting reason. Note that we paraphrased (or put into our own words) the major reasons to some extent. You will find that the longer and more complex a reason, the more useful paraphrasing will be to your accurately identifying the reasons.

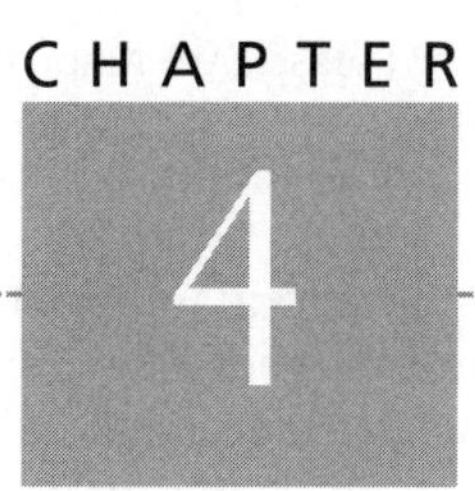

CHAPTER 4

What Words or Phrases Are Ambiguous?

Chapters 2 and 3 of this book help you identify the basic structural elements in any message. At this point, if you can locate a writer's or speaker's conclusion and reasons, you are progressing rapidly toward the ultimate goal of forming your own rational decisions. Your next step is to put this structural picture into even clearer focus.

While identifying the conclusion and reasons gives you the basic visible structure, you still need to examine the precise *meaning* of these parts before you can react fairly to the ideas being presented. Now you need to pay special attention to the details of the language.

Identifying the precise meaning of key words or phrases is an essential step in deciding whether to agree with someone's opinion. If you fail to check for the meaning of crucial terms and phrases, you may react to an opinion the author never intended.

Let's see why knowing the meaning of a communicator's terms is so important.

> Tourism is getting out of control. Tourism can be good for the economy, but it can also harm the locale and its residents. We need to do more to regulate tourism. If we keep allowing these people to do whatever they please, surely we as residents will suffer.

Notice that it is very hard to know what to think about this argument until we know more about the kinds of regulations that the writer has in mind. A quota for tourists? A set of rules about the behavior expected of tourists?

We just do not know what to think until we know more about these regulations the writer is suggesting.

This example illustrates an important point: You cannot react to an argument unless you understand the meanings (explicit or implied) of crucial terms and phrases. How these are interpreted will often affect the acceptability of the reasoning. Consequently, before you can determine the extent to which you wish to accept one conclusion or another, you must first attempt to discover the precise meaning of the conclusion and the reasons. While their meaning typically *appears* obvious, it often is not.

The discovery and clarification of meaning require conscious, step-by-step procedures. This chapter suggests one set of such procedures. It focuses on the following question:

? *Critical Question:* ***What words or phrases are ambiguous?***

THE CONFUSING FLEXIBILITY OF WORDS

Our language is highly complex. If each word had only one potential meaning about which we all agreed, effective communication would be more likely. However, most words have more than one meaning.

Consider the multiple meanings of such words as *freedom*, *obscenity*, and *fairness*. These multiple meanings can create serious problems in determining the worth of an argument. For example, when someone argues that a magazine should not be published because it is *obscene*, you cannot evaluate the argument until you know what the writer means by *obscene*. In this brief argument, it is easy to find the conclusion and the supporting reason, but the quality of the reasoning is difficult to judge because of the ambiguous use of *obscene*. A warning: *We often misunderstand what we read or hear because we presume that the meaning of words is obvious.*

Whenever you are reading or listening, force yourself to *search for ambiguity*; otherwise, you may simply miss the point. A term or phrase is ambiguous when its meaning is so uncertain in the context of the argument we are examining that we need further clarification before we can judge the adequacy of the reasoning.

When any of us is ambiguous, we have not necessarily done something either unfair or improper. In fact, many documents, like constitutions, are intentionally left ambiguous so that the document can evolve as different meanings of key terms, like "liberty" and "bear arms," become practical necessities. Indeed, because we rely on words to get our points across when we communicate, there is no way to avoid ambiguity. But what can and should be avoided is ambiguity in an argument. When someone is trying to persuade us to believe or do something, that person has a responsibility to clarify any potential ambiguity before we consider the worth of the reasoning.

LOCATING KEY TERMS AND PHRASES

The first step in determining which terms or phrases are ambiguous is to use the stated issue as a clue for possible key terms. Key terms or phrases will be those terms that may have more than one plausible meaning within the context of the issue; that is, terms that you know must be clarified before you can decide to agree or disagree with the communicator. To illustrate the potential benefit of checking the meaning of terminology in the stated issue, let's examine several issues:

1. Does a high income produce happiness?
2. Do reality shows create a misleading picture of how we live?
3. Is the incidence of rape in college residence halls increasing?

***Attention:** Ambiguity refers to the existence of multiple possible meanings for a word or phrase.*

Each of these stated issues contains phrases that writers or speakers will have to make clear before you will be able to evaluate their response to the issue. Each of the following phrases is potentially ambiguous: "high income," "happiness," "misleading picture," and "incidence of rape." Thus, when you read an essay responding to these issues, you have to pay close attention to how the author has defined these terms.

The next step in determining which terms or phrases are ambiguous is to identify what words or phrases seem crucial in determining how well the author's reasons support her conclusion; that is, to identify the *key* terms in the reasoning structure. Once you locate these terms, you can determine whether their meaning is ambiguous.

When searching for key terms and phrases, you should keep in mind why you are looking. Someone wants you to accept a conclusion. Therefore, you are looking for only those terms or phrases that will affect whether you accept the conclusion. *So, look for them in the reasons and conclusion.* Terms and phrases that are not included in the basic reasoning structure can thus be "dumped from your pan."

Another useful guide for searching for key terms and phrases is to keep in mind the following rule: The more abstract a word or phrase, the more likely it is to be susceptible to multiple interpretations.

To avoid being unclear in our use of the term *abstract*, we define it here in the following way: A term becomes more and more abstract as it refers less and less to particular, specific instances. Thus, the words *equality*, *responsibility*, *pornography*, and *aggression* are much more abstract than are the phrases "having equal access to necessities of life," "directly causing an event," "pictures of male and female genitals," and "doing deliberate physical

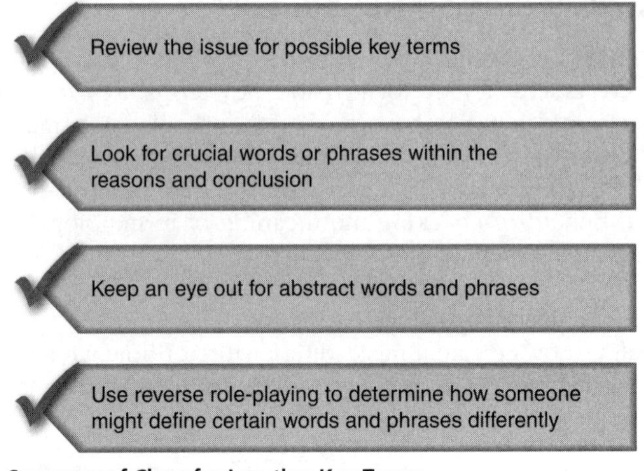

Summary of Clues for Locating Key Terms

harm to another person." These phrases provide a much more concrete picture and are therefore less ambiguous.

You can also locate potential important ambiguous phrases by *reverse role-playing*. Ask yourself, if you were to *adopt a position contrary to the author's*, would you choose to define certain terms or phrases differently? If so, you have identified a possible ambiguity. For example, someone who sees dog shows as desirable is likely to define "cruelty to animals" quite differently from someone who sees them as undesirable.

CHECKING FOR AMBIGUITY

You now know where to look for ambiguous terms or phrases. The next step is to focus on each term or phrase and ask yourself, "Do I understand its meaning?" To answer this very important question, you will need to overcome several major obstacles.

One obstacle is assuming that you and the author mean the same thing. Thus, you need to begin your search by avoiding mind reading. You need to get into the habit of asking, "What do you mean by that?" instead of, "I know just what you mean." A second obstacle is assuming that terms have a single, obvious definition. Many terms do not. Thus, always ask, "Could any of the words or phrases have a different meaning?"

You can be certain you have identified an especially important unclear term by performing the following test. If you can express two or more alternative meanings for a term, each of which makes sense in the context of the argument, and if the extent to which a reason would support a conclusion is affected by which meaning is assumed, then you have located a significant ambiguity. Thus, a good test for determining whether you have identified an important ambiguity is to *substitute* the alternative meanings into the reasoning structure and see whether changing the meaning *makes a difference* in how well a reason supports the conclusion.

USING THIS CRITICAL QUESTION

The preceding paragraph deserves your full attention. It is spelling out a procedure for putting this critical question about ambiguity to work. Once you have followed the procedure, you can demonstrate to yourself or anyone else why the reasoning needs more work. Try as you might to want to believe what is being said, you just cannot, as a critical thinker, agree with the reasoning until the ambiguity that affects the reasoning is repaired.

DETERMINING AMBIGUITY

Let's now apply the above-mentioned hints to help us determine which key terms a communicator has left unclear. *Remember:* As we do this exercise, keep asking, "What does the author mean by that?" and pay particular attention to abstract terms.

We will start with a simple reasoning structure: an advertisement.

OurBrand Sleep Aid: Works great in just 30 min.

ISSUE: What sleep aid should you buy?

CONCLUSION (implied): *Buy OurBrand Sleep Aid.*

REASON: Works great in 30 min.

The phrases "Buy OurBrand Sleep Aid" and "in 30 min" seem quite concrete and self-evident. But, how about "works great?" Is the meaning obvious? We think not. How do we know? Let's perform a test together. Could "works great" have more than one meaning? Yes. It could mean the pill makes you drowsy. It could mean the pill completely knocks you out such that you will have difficulty waking up the next morning. Or it could have many other meanings. Isn't it true that you would be more eager to follow the advice of the advertisement if the pill worked great, meaning it works precisely as you want it to work? Thus, the ambiguity is significant because it affects the degree to which you might be persuaded by the advertisement.

Advertising is often full of ambiguity. Advertisers intentionally engage in ambiguity to persuade you that their products are superior to those of their competitors. Here are some sample advertising claims that are ambiguous. See if you can identify alternative, plausible meanings for the italicized words or phrases.

No-Pain is the *extra-strength* pain reliever.

Here is a book at last that shows you how to find and keep a *good man.*

In each case, the advertiser hoped that you would assign the most attractive meaning to the ambiguous words. Critical reading can sometimes protect you from making purchasing decisions that you would later regret.

Let's now look at a more complicated example of ambiguity. Remember to begin by identifying the issue, conclusion, and reasons. Resist the temptation to make note of the unclear meaning of any word and all words. Only the ambiguity **in the reasoning** is crucial to critical thinkers.

> We absolutely must put limits on tanning. Tanning is a substantial health risk with severe consequences. Studies have shown that those who tan are at a higher risk of skin diseases as a result of tanning.

Let's examine the reasoning for any words or phrases that would affect our willingness to accept it.

First, let's inspect the issue for terms we will want the author to make clear. Certainly, we would not be able to agree or disagree with this author's conclusion until she has indicated what she means by *tanning*. Does she mean tanning outdoors or artificial tanning? Thus, we will want to check how clearly she has defined it in her reasoning.

Next, let's list all key terms and phrases in the conclusion and reasons: "health risk," "severe consequences," "studies have shown," "those who tan are at a higher risk," "skin diseases," and "we should put limits on tanning." Let's take a close look at a few of these to determine whether they could have different meanings that might make a difference in how we would react to the reasoning.

First, her conclusion is ambiguous. Exactly what does it mean to "put limits on tanning"? Does it mean to prevent people from using artificial tanning devices, or might it mean putting a limit on the amount of time spent tanning? Before you could decide whether to agree with the speaker or writer, you would first have to decide what she wants us to believe.

Next, she argues that "those who tan are at a higher risk of skin diseases." We have already talked about how we are not sure what she means by "those who tan," but what does she mean by "skin diseases"? She could mean any number of irritations that can occur from sun exposure, or she could be talking about something as severe as skin cancer. It is significant to know which of these she was addressing if she wanted to convince you of the dangers of tanning and her conclusion to limit it. Try to create a mental picture of what these phrases represent. If you can't, the phrases are ambiguous. If different images would cause you to react to the reasons differently, you have identified an important ambiguity.

Now, check the other phrases we listed earlier. Do they not also need to be clarified? You can see that if you accept this writer's argument without requiring her to clarify these ambiguous phrases, you will not have understood what you agreed to believe.

CONTEXT AND AMBIGUITY

Writers and speakers only rarely define their key terms. Thus, typically your only guide to the meaning of an ambiguous statement is the context in which the words are used. By *context*, we mean the writer's or speaker's background, traditional uses of the term within the particular controversy, and the words and statements preceding and following the possible ambiguity. All three elements provide clues to the meaning of a potential key term or phrase.

If you were to see the term *human rights* in an essay, you should immediately ask yourself, "What rights are those?" If you examine the context and find that the writer is a leading member of the Norwegian government, it is a good bet that the human rights she has in mind are the rights to be employed, receive free health care, and obtain adequate housing. An American senator might mean something very different by human rights. She could have in mind freedoms of speech, religion, travel, and peaceful assembly. Notice that the two versions of human rights are not necessarily consistent. A country could guarantee one form of human rights and at the same time violate the other. You must try to clarify such terms by examining their context.

Writers frequently make clear their assumed meaning for a term by their arguments. The following paragraph is an example:

> The amusement park has given great satisfaction to most of its customers. More than half of the people surveyed agreed that the park had a wide variety of games and rides and that they would return to the park soon.

The phrase "given great satisfaction" is potentially ambiguous because it could have a variety of meanings. However, the writer's argument makes clear that in this context, "given great satisfaction" means enjoying a variety of games and rides.

Note that, even in this case, you would want some further clarification before you travel to this park because "a wide variety of games" is ambiguous. Wouldn't you want to know perhaps how many rides or games there were, or what some of them were? It is possible that while there was a wide variety of games, all of them were outdated or not popular anymore?

USING THIS CRITICAL QUESTION

The critical question focusing on ambiguity provides you with a fair-minded basis for disagreeing with the reasoning. If you and the person trying to persuade you are using different meanings for key terms in the reasoning, you would have to work out those disagreements first before you could accept the reasoning being offered to you.

Examine the context carefully to determine the meaning of key terms and phrases. If the meaning remains uncertain, you have located an important ambiguity. If the meaning is clear and you disagree with it, then you should be wary of any reasoning that involves that term or phrase.

AMBIGUITY, DEFINITIONS, AND THE DICTIONARY

It should be obvious from the preceding discussion that to locate and clarify ambiguity, you must be aware of the possible meanings of words. Meanings usually come in one of three forms: synonyms, examples, and what we will call "definition by specific criteria." For example, one could offer at least three different definitions of *anxiety*:

1. Anxiety is feeling nervous (*synonym*).
2. Anxiety is what the candidate experienced when he turned on the television to watch the election returns (*example*).
3. Anxiety is a subjective feeling of discomfort accompanied by increased sensitivity of the autonomic nervous system (*specific criteria*).

For critical evaluation of most controversial issues, synonyms and examples are inadequate. They fail to tell you the specific properties that are crucial for an unambiguous understanding of the term. Useful definitions are those that specify criteria for usage—the more specific, the better.

Where do you go for your definitions? One obvious and very important source is your dictionary. However, dictionary definitions frequently consist of synonyms, examples, or incomplete specifications of criteria for usage. These definitions often do not adequately define the use of a term in a particular essay. In such cases, you must discover possible meanings from the context of the passage, or from what else you know about the topic. We suggest you keep a dictionary handy, but keep in mind that the appropriate definition may not be there.

Let's take a closer look at some of the inadequacies of a dictionary definition. Examine the following paragraph.

> The quality of education at this university is not declining. In my interviews, I found that an overwhelming majority of the students and instructors responded that they saw no decline in the quality of education here.

It is clearly important to know what is meant by "quality of education" in the given paragraph. If you look up the word *quality* in the dictionary, you will find many meanings, the most appropriate, given this context, being *excellence* or *superiority*. *Excellence* and *superiority* are synonyms for quality—and they are equally abstract. You still need to know precisely what is meant by *excellence* or *superiority*. How do you know whether education is high in quality or excellence? Ideally, you would want the writer to tell you precisely what *behaviors* she is referring to when she uses the phrase "quality of education." Can you think of some different ways that the phrase might be defined? The following list presents some possible definitions of *quality of education*:

average grade-point of students

ability of students to think critically

number of professors who have doctoral degrees

amount of work usually required to pass an exam

Each of these definitions suggests a different way to measure quality; each specifies a different criterion. Each provides a concrete way in which the term could be used. Note also that each of these definitions will affect the degree to which you will want to agree with the author's reasoning. For example, if you believe that "quality" should refer to the ability of students to think critically, and most of the students in the interviews are defining it as how much work is required to pass an exam, the reason would not *necessarily* support the conclusion. Exams may not require the ability to think critically.

Thus, in many arguments, you will not be able to find adequate dictionary definitions, and the context may not make the meaning clear. One way to discover possible alternative meanings is to try to create a mental picture of what the words represent. If you cannot do so, then you probably have identified an important ambiguity. Let's apply such a test to the following example:

> Our company has had many competent employees. If you join our staff, you will start immediately at the rate we discussed with, of course, added benefits. I hope you consider all these factors in making your employment decision.

This is clearly an argument to persuade someone to work at his or her place of employment. The reasons are the salary and "added benefits." Can you create a single clear mental picture of "added benefits"? We each have some such idea, but it is highly unlikely that the ideas are identical; indeed, they may be quite different. Do "added benefits" refer to health care insurance or a new corner office? For us to evaluate the argument, we would need to know more about the meaning the writer has for "added benefits." Thus, we have located an important ambiguity.

AMBIGUITY AND LOADED LANGUAGE

Which do you believe is a greater threat to society: *global warming* or *climate change?*

Would you be more likely to vote for *tax relief* than for a *tax cut?*

Would you be more willing to vote for the reduction of *death taxes* than *estate taxes?*

Research shows that people have different emotional reactions to the italicized terms in the above-given sentences even though the terms have similar definitions. American citizens respond more positively to tax relief than to tax cut and are more likely to support the reduction of death taxes than estate taxes. Different emotional reactions to selected terms and phrases can greatly influence how we respond to arguments. Terms and phrases have both denotative and connotative meanings. The denotative meaning refers to the agreed-upon explicit descriptive referents for use of the word, the kinds of meanings we have emphasized thus far in this chapter. There is another important meaning, however, that you need to attend to. The connotative meaning is the emotional associations that we have to a term or phrase. For example the phrase "raising taxes" may have similar denotative meanings to people but each meaning triggers very different emotional reactions. Terms that trigger strong emotional reactions are called *loaded terms*. Their ability to move us outweighs their descriptive meanings. Such terms make trouble for critical thinking because they short-circuit thought and trick the mind by directly contacting its emotional circuits while bypassing the descriptive meaning circuits.

Ambiguity is not always an accident. Those trying to persuade you are often quite aware that words have multiple meanings. Furthermore, they know that certain of those meanings carry with them heavy emotional baggage. Words like *sacrifice* and *justice* have multiple meanings, and some of those meanings are loaded in the sense that they stimulate certain emotions in us. Anyone trying to use language to lead us by the heart can take advantage of these probable emotions. They can do so by using language that heightens our positive emotional reactions or cools our negative emotional reactions to ideas.

For example, the American military officials who control prisons in Afghanistan and Guantanamo are eager to avoid the appearance that these prisons encourage a large number of suicides among the prisoners. Yet a large number of prisoners do take their own lives. The military have to count those deaths somehow. So they have created categories like "self-inflicted hazardous incidents" that permit them to acknowledge the deaths without putting them into the category of suicides. Here the ambiguity of "self-inflicted hazardous incidents" is far from accidental; it is meant to defuse emotional reactions to the ideas it references.

Political language is often loaded and ambiguous. For example, *welfare* is often how we refer to governmental help to those we don't like; when help from the government goes to groups we like, we call it *assistance to the poor*. The following table consists of political terms and the intended emotional impact.

Ambiguous Political Language

Term	Emotional Impact
Restoring	Approval of proposed tax
Fairness	Changes
Terrorist	Wild, crazy, uncivilized
Reform	Desirable changes

All the terms in the table are ambiguous and have potentially influential emotional associations. As critical thinkers, we must be sensitive to their intended emotional impact and the role of ambiguity in encouraging that impact. Be alert to how terms make you FEEL! Are those feelings blinding you to some important feature of the term? By clarifying the denotative meaning and searching for alternative meanings of terms such as *reform*, we can safeguard ourselves against easy emotional commitments to arguments we would otherwise question. After all, even the most dangerous political change is in some sense a "reform."

Norman Solomon's *The Power of Babble* provides a colorful illustration of how successful politicians use ambiguous language to persuade others. Note that Solomon has conveniently placed key ambiguous terms in alphabetical order for us.

> America is back, and bipartisan—biting the bullet with competitiveness, diplomacy, efficiency, empowerment, end games, and environmentalism, along with faith in the Founding Fathers, freedom's blessings, free markets and free peoples, and most of all, God. Our great heritage has held the line for human rights, individual initiative, justice, kids, leadership, liberty, loyalty, mainstream values, the marketplace, measured responses, melting pots, the middle class, military reform, moderates, modernization, moral standards, national security, and Old Glory. Opportunity comes from optimism, patriotism, peace through strength, the people, pluralism, and points of light. Pragmatism and the power of prayer make for principle while the private sector protects the public interest. Realism can mean recycling, self-discipline, and the spirit of '76, bring stability and standing tall for strategic interests and streamlined taxation. Uncle Sam has been undaunted ever since Valley Forge, with values venerated by veterans; vigilance, vigor, vision, voluntarism, and Western values. (p. 3)

LIMITS OF YOUR RESPONSIBILITY TO CLARIFY AMBIGUITY

After you have attempted to identify and clarify ambiguity, what can you do if you are still uncertain about the meaning of certain key ideas? What is a reasonable next step? We suggest you ignore any reason containing ambiguity that makes it impossible to judge the acceptability of the reason. It is your responsibility as an active learner to ask questions that clarify ambiguity. However, your responsibility stops at that point. It is the writer or speaker who is trying to convince you of something. Her role as a persuader requires her to respond to your concerns about possible ambiguity.

You are not required to react to unclear ideas or options. If a friend tells you that you should enroll in a class because it "really is different," but cannot tell you how it is different, then you have no basis for agreeing or disagreeing with the advice. No one has the right to be believed if he cannot provide you with a clear picture of his reasoning.

Here is one last example of the power of ambiguity. Consider the billions of dollars at issue in this eventual court struggle. An insurance policy covering a leaseholder at the World Trade Center contains protection limits for "each event." After 9/11, the leaseholder asks his insurance company to pay tens of billions of dollars to *the survivors of each employee* who was killed in the 9/11 tragedy. His understanding of an insurance event is each death. The insurance company replied that there was only one event—the World Trade Center disaster—and that the policy contained a $3.5 billion per-event insurance maximum.

AMBIGUITY AND YOUR OWN WRITING AND SPEAKING

Imagine you are in the midst of a heated conversation with your roommate, which concludes with the statement: "You wouldn't understand. Your family is well-off!" After reading this chapter, you know that the word *well-off* is a loaded term, full of ambiguity. Each person who uses the word applies her own cultural, ideological, and experiential meaning to the term. *Well-off* to a newly naturalized refugee family may connote regular work and the ability to meet basic needs. To another person, it may mean a stable, salaried position. To another, nothing short of six figures is *well-off*. With the nearly limitless legitimate variations of this term, it's easy to see why true communication can be difficult. In the midst of a conversation, two people at least have the immediate opportunity to bring potential ambiguities to the surface and clear them up before continuing. Not so for a writer.

Writing alone with only your laptop to keep you company, you face a great challenge. In the solitude of writing, you must overcome the temptation to believe that a definition is self-evident. It's easy to forget the overwhelming diversity of cultures, experiences, and ideologies, all of which add layers of meaning to words. To help you avoid this obstacle, we have some suggestions.

Keeping Your Eye Out for Ambiguity

Effective writers strive for clarity. They review what they intend to say several times, looking for any statements that might be ambiguous. Because the meaning is clear to the writer, the task of identifying what may be unclear to readers is not easy.

To help you with this task, apply *reverse role-playing*, a process we discussed earlier in the chapter. When you are concerned about a potential ambiguity, reverse role-playing provides an opportunity to be creative. Try to adopt the frame of mind of a person from a different culture or a person with a different political ideology. Exploring your argument from another person's perspective may draw your attention to ambiguous spots you did not notice previously.

During your initial research, we urged you to immerse yourself in the ongoing discussion of your issue in popular and academic publications. Another option for testing whether your key phrases are ambiguous is to return to this research. Do authors in the ongoing discussion debate over specific terms or use the same terms differently? If you notice a debate over a term, check your writing project. Did you employ the term or a similar one? If so, you now know that you should take care to explicitly state how you are using the word.

Writing need not be a completely solitary activity. Our last suggestion to avoid presuming your key terms are obvious is to start a dialogue. Share your conclusion and reasons with others, such as friends and classmates. Encourage them to ask questions. Observe whether they use the term in a manner significantly different than you do.

Before you determine whether a potential ambiguity needs to be clarified, take a moment to think about your audience. Some audiences share a common set of ideas and language. If you used the word *torque* with a group of physicists, the term has a specific and well-known definition, that is, a specific and measurable type of force. If you use the same word with a group of motorcycle enthusiasts, the term has another specific and related meaning. With this audience, however, the term is mostly limited to the power of their vehicle's engine. When the motorcyclist is describing the advantages of his bike to another rider, he does not need to qualify his use. Thinking about the characteristics of your intended audience can help you decide where ambiguities need to be clarified. If your writing is intended for a specialized audience, they may adequately understand jargon or specific abstractions that would be very ambiguous to a general audience. Another extension of this comment is shared coursework. In your senior psychology seminar, for example, you need not painstakingly define psychoanalysis or regression as you would to an audience without this common coursework.

Alternatively, if your writing is intended for a general audience, keep in mind that your specialized language may be lost on them and you may lose readers quickly and possibly never regain their attention.

Once you have determined that a word in your argument is ambiguous, you have to clarify. Before you can persuade someone to accept your conclusion and reasons, you must make sure that your audience is reacting to the same conclusion and reasons. When you fear ambiguity of expression, carefully define your terms.

PRACTICE EXERCISES

? *Critical Question:* ***What words or phrases are ambiguous?***

In the following passages, identify examples of ambiguity. Try to explain why the examples harm the reasoning.

Passage 1

School dress codes are limits put on inappropriate clothing to help keep the learning environment focused. It can be quite a distraction for students if a classmate wears inappropriate clothing. The use of a dress code during school is not preventing freedom of expression. Unlike required uniform dress codes, the dress code still allows for students to choose what they wear as long as it is not deemed inappropriate.

Passage 2

We should treat drug use in the same way we treat speech and religion, as a fundamental right. No one has to ingest any drug he does not want, just as no one has to read a particular book. The only reason the state assumes control over such matters is to subjugate its citizens—by shielding them from temptations as befits children.

Passage 3

The government needs to drastically reduce immigration to the United States. The United States is already overpopulated, and we're suffering consequences, such as high unemployment and serious water pollution. Also immigrants endanger our American culture.

Sample Responses

For the first practice passage, our sample response shares with you an in-depth "thinking aloud" model of the critical thinking process we have been describing in this chapter and the previous two chapters.

Passage 1

- *If this passage has any significant ambiguity,* Asking the Right Questions (ARQ) *said that I'll find it in the issue, conclusion, or reasons. So my first step will be to find those parts of the argument. Neither the issue nor the conclusion is explicitly stated in this passage. No indicator words are present. I'll have to try other tools to identify the issue and conclusion. To find the issue,* ARQ *suggests that I ask, "What is the author reacting to?" Dress codes, I guess. Whether they are a good idea. Okay, so I'll word that idea as a question: "Should schools have a dress code?" All of the sentences in this passage are trying to convince me that we should have a dress code, so the conclusion must be, "Yes, schools should have a dress code."*
- *Again, there are no indicator words to help me find the reasons. So I'll try something else. To find the reasons, I need to put myself in the author's shoes and ask, "Why should schools have a dress code?" I can deduce two reasons from the passage: First, inappropriate clothing distracts from learning, and second, dress codes do not violate freedom of expression.*
- *Now that I have broken the argument down into its most basic elements, I can start the process of finding significant ambiguity. I'll start by identifying the key words or phrases in the issue, conclusion, and reasons*

because these words and phrases are crucial to the argument. They may have more than one plausible meaning within the context. For instance, they could be abstract terms or loaded language. "Inappropriate clothing" is definitely an important element of the argument. And the author never tells me what qualifies as inappropriate. I wonder if there are other possible meanings for the term.

- *"Inappropriate clothing," as far I'm concerned, is clothing with hurtful or insulting text. I'd prohibit them from schools too! T-shirts that make fun of people are definitely inappropriate. It's pretty clear to me. Of course,* ARQ *said that I might think the definition of a term is obvious, even if it's not. So I should keep questioning. Could this phrase have a different meaning?*
- *One of the clues that* ARQ *suggested was to pay attention to abstract words like* obscenity *and* responsibility. *These words are abstract—and also ambiguous—because they don't have a specific definition or set of criteria for us.* Inappropriate *similarly does not have a specific definition or set of criteria in this passage. The author never says that* inappropriate *means hurtful text on T-shirts. I just assumed that meaning because I think those T-shirts are inappropriate. The author also doesn't say that inappropriate means skirts of a certain length or wearing pants so low that one can see a guy's boxers. The term is starting to seem a little less obvious than I originally thought.*
- *Before I can be sure, I want to try the reverse role-playing suggestion. How would an opponent of this conclusion define the term* inappropriate clothing? *Opponents of this argument would probably argue that dress codes DO prohibit freedom of expression. What might students want to express with their clothing? Political messages are often seen on T-shirts. I've seen teenagers wearing T-shirts with antiwar slogans or slogans supporting their favorite presidential candidate. An opponent of dress codes probably would fear that students would be denied the right to voice their opinions about important issues.*
- *Wow. Now I'm stuck. If the author is talking about messages on T-shirts that hurt people, I agree. Let's prohibit them. But if the author's talking about limiting students' ability to voice their political opinions, I strongly disagree. I can't come to a decision about this issue until the ambiguity is resolved.*

Passage 2

ISSUE: *Should the state regulate drug use?*

CONCLUSION: *Drug use should not be regulated by the state.*

REASONS:
1. *Just as freedom of speech and religion, drug use is a fundamental right.*
2. *State control subjugates citizens by not permitting them to take responsibility for voluntary acts.*

What are the key phrases in this reasoning? They are: "drug use," "fundamental right," and "subjugate citizens." You would first want to determine the meaning of each of these phrases. Is what is meant by "drug use" clear? No. The limited context provided fails to reveal an adequate definition. If "drug use" refers to the ingestion of drugs that are not considered highly addictive, such as marijuana, wouldn't you be more likely to accept the reasoning than if the author included heroin within her definition of drugs? Can you tell from the argument whether the author is referring to all drugs or only to a subset of currently regulated drugs? To be able to agree or to disagree with the author requires in this instance a more careful definition of what is meant by "drug use." Notice that "fundamental right" and "subjugate citizens" need further clarification before you can decide whether to agree with the author.

CHAPTER

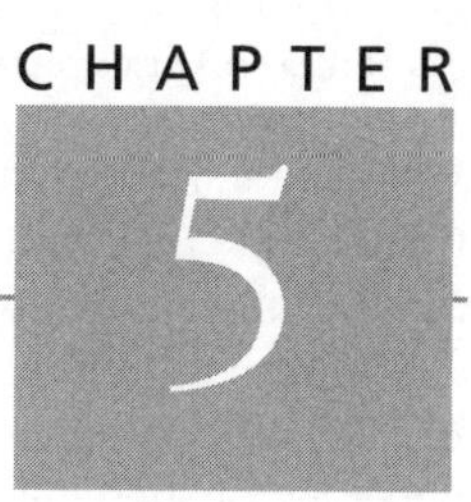

What Are the Value and Descriptive Assumptions?

Anyone trying to convince you to believe a particular position will make an attempt to present reasons consistent with that position. Hence, at first glance, almost every argument appears to "make sense." The visible structure looks good. But the visible, stated reasons are not the only ideas that serve to prove or support the conclusion. Hidden or unstated beliefs may be at least as significant in understanding the argument. Let's examine the importance of these unstated ideas by considering the following argument.

> Local law enforcement needs to do more to impose consequences for littering. Obviously, people are not taking enough initiative on their own to follow the laws; therefore, city police have to do something. How can we expect change without enforcement?

The reason—at first glance—supports the conclusion. If the city expects change in the behavior of its citizens, it follows that the city's law enforcement should have to enforce that change. But it is also possible that the reason given can be true and yet not necessarily support the conclusion. What if you believe that it is the individual's responsibility—not the collective responsibility of the government—to curb the extent of littering? If so, from your perspective, the reason no longer supports the conclusion. This reasoning is convincing to you only if you agree with certain unstated ideas that the writer has taken for granted. In this case, one idea taken for granted is that one value, collective responsibility, is more desirable than the other, individual responsibility.

In all arguments, there will be certain ideas taken for granted by the writer. Typically, these ideas will not be stated. You will have to find them by reading between the lines. These ideas are important invisible links in the reasoning structure, the glue that holds the entire argument together. Such ideas answer the very important question of, "What idea is necessary to logically connect a reason to a conclusion?" The necessity of such links should seem obvious. Without such links, how could one decide which of thousands of ideas qualify as reasons? Until you supply these links, you cannot truly understand the argument.

If you miss the hidden links, you will often find yourself believing something that, had you been more reflective, you would never have accepted. *Remember*: The visible surface of an argument will almost always be dressed in its best clothes because the person presenting the argument wishes to encourage you to make the argument your own. This chapter can be particularly useful to you as a critical thinker because it prepares you to look at the full argument, not just its more attractive features.

As another illustration, consider why you should work hard to master the skills and attitudes contained in this book. There are all kinds of reasons why you should not learn critical thinking. Careful thought is much more demanding of our energies than another decision-making approach like flipping a coin or asking the nearest self-confident expert what you should think and do. But this text is encouraging you to learn critical thinking. We are telling you that critical thinking is advantageous for you.

Our advice is based on some invisible beliefs, and if you do not share those beliefs, our advice should not be followed. Critical thinkers believe that such values as autonomy, curiosity, and reasonableness are among the most important of human objectives. The end-product of critical thinking is someone who is open to multiple points of view, assesses those perspectives with reason, and then uses that assessment to make decisions about what to believe and what actions to take. We trust that you like that portrayal of life and, consequently, that you will want to be a critical thinker.

When trying to understand someone, your task is similar in many ways to having to reproduce a magic trick without having seen how the magician did the trick. You see the handkerchief go into the hat and the rabbit come out, but you are not aware of the magician's hidden maneuvers. To understand the trick, you must discover these maneuvers. Likewise, in arguments, you must discover the hidden maneuvers, which, in actuality, are unstated ideas. We shall refer to these unstated ideas as assumptions. To fully understand an argument, you must identify the assumptions.

Assumptions are:

1. hidden or unstated (in most cases);
2. taken for granted;
3. influential in determining the conclusion; and
4. potentially deceptive.

This chapter will show you how to discover assumptions. But identifying assumptions is more valuable than just the positive impact it has on your

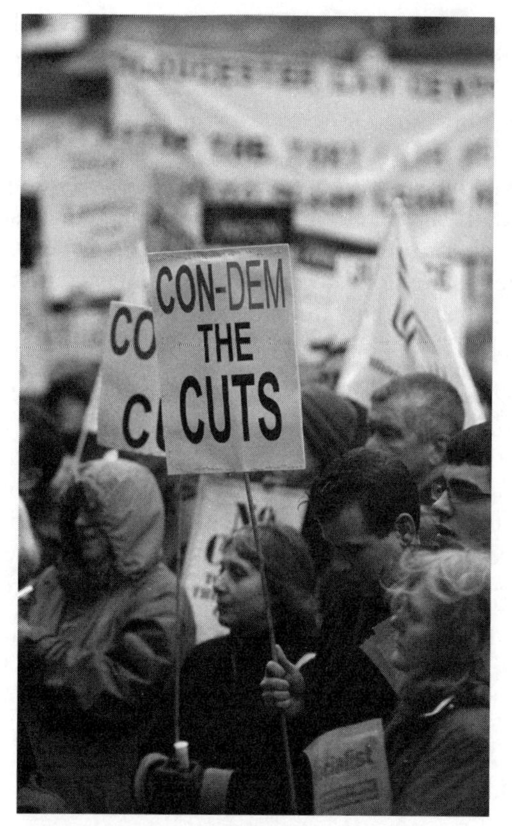

Assumptions in Bunches © Getty Images

own reasoning. Critical thinking necessarily involves other people who are concerned about the same issues as you are. When you identify assumptions and make them explicit in your interactions with others, you make a tremendous contribution to the quality of the reasoning in our community as well.

For instance, the Associated Press recently ran an account of a study by the St. Louis Federal Reserve Bank. The study concluded that good-looking people tend to make more money and get promoted more often than those who are just average looking. As a critical thinker, you can question the assumptions behind such a report and, in so doing, prevent yourself from quickly embracing arguments that use such data to support the conclusions. Democracy badly needs this kind of cautious reflection.

Critical Question: ***What are the assumptions?***

GENERAL GUIDE FOR IDENTIFYING ASSUMPTIONS

When you seek assumptions, where and how should you look? Numerous assumptions exist in any book, discussion, or article, but you need to be concerned about relatively few. As you remember, the visible structure of an argument consists of reasons and conclusions. But, you are interested only in assumptions that affect the quality of this structure. You can restrict your search for assumptions, therefore, to the structure you have already learned to identify.

In particular, there are two places to look for assumptions. Look for assumptions needed for the reason(s) to support the conclusions (linkage assumptions) and look for ones necessary for a reason to be true. We first introduce you to value assumptions and then to descriptive assumptions. Both are extremely influential in shaping arguments.

***Attention:* Look for both value and descriptive assumptions in the movement from reasons to the conclusions.**

Note that reasons and the conclusion are also the places where we search for significant ambiguity. Once again, we are showing great respect for the importance of the reasons and the conclusion in a speech or an essay.

***Attention:* An assumption is a belief, usually unstated, that is taken for granted and supports the explicit reasoning.**

VALUE CONFLICTS AND ASSUMPTIONS

Why is it that some very reasonable people shout that abortion is murder, while other equally reasonable observers see abortion as humane? Have you ever wondered why every U.S. president, regardless of his political beliefs, eventually gets involved in a dispute with the press over publication of government information that he would prefer not to share? How can some highly intelligent observers attack the publication of sexually explicit magazines and others defend their publication as the ultimate test of our Bill of Rights?

One extremely important reason for these different conclusions is the existence of value conflicts, or the differing values that stem from different frames of reference. For ethical or prescriptive arguments, an individual's values influence the reasons he provides and, consequently, his conclusion. In fact, the reasons will logically support the conclusion only if the value assumption is added to the reasoning. The argument that follows illustrates the role of a value assumption in a prescriptive argument.

> We should not legalize recreational drugs. Such drugs cause too much street violence and other crimes.

Note that the reason only logically supports the conclusion if one takes for granted the idea that it is more important to value public safety than it is to value individual responsibility. Value assumptions are very important assumptions for such arguments because they are directing the reasoning from behind a screen. The person trying to communicate with you may or may not be aware of these assumptions. You should make it a habit to identify the value assumptions on which the reasons are based.

By *value assumption*, we mean a taken-for-granted belief about the relative desirability of certain competing values. When authors take a position on a social controversy, they typically prefer one value over another value—they have value priorities or preferences. To identify these priorities, you need to have a good grasp of what is meant by *values*. Consequently, this is a good time to review the introduction of values in Chapter 1.

FROM VALUES TO VALUE ASSUMPTIONS

To identify value assumptions, we must go beyond a simple listing of values. Others share many of your values. For example, wouldn't almost anyone claim that flexibility, cooperation, and honesty are desirable?

Look again at the definition, and you will immediately see that, by definition, most values will be on everyone's list. Because many values are shared, values by themselves are not a powerful guide to understanding. What leads you to answer a prescriptive question differently from someone else is the relative intensity with which you hold specific values.

That we attach different levels of intensity to specific values can be appreciated by thinking about responses to controversies when pairs of values collide or conflict. While it is not very enlightening to discover that most people value both competition and cooperation, we do gain a more complete understanding of prescriptive choices as we discover who prefers competition to cooperation when the two values conflict.

A person's preference for particular values is often unstated, but that value preference, nevertheless, will have a major impact on her conclusion and on how she chooses to defend it. These unstated assertions about value priorities function as value assumptions. Some refer to these assumptions as *value judgments*. Recognition of relative support for conflicting values or sets of values provides you with both an improved understanding of what you are reading and a basis for eventual evaluation of prescriptive arguments.

Attention: ***A value assumption is an implicit preference for one value over another in a particular context. We use value preferences and value priorities as synonyms.***

When you have found a person's value preference in a particular argument, you should not expect that same person to necessarily have the same value priority when discussing a different controversy. A person does not have the same value priorities without regard to the issue being discussed.

The context and factual issues associated with a controversy also greatly influence how far we're willing to go with a particular value preference. We hold our value preferences only up to a point. Thus, for example, those who prefer freedom of choice over the welfare of the community in most situations (such as wearing clothing that displays an image of the flag) may shift that value preference when they see the possibility of too much damage to the welfare of the community (such as in the case of the right of a person to give a racist speech). In other words, value assumptions are very contextual; they apply in one setting, but we may make quite a different value priority when the specifics of the prescriptive issue change.

TYPICAL VALUE CONFLICTS

If you are aware of typical conflicts, you can more quickly recognize the assumptions being made by a writer when she reaches a particular conclusion. We have listed some of the more common value conflicts that occur in ethical issues and have provided you with examples of controversies in which these value conflicts are likely to be evident. You can use this list as a starting point when you are trying to identify important value assumptions.

As you identify value conflicts, you will often find that there are several that seem important in shaping conclusions with respect to particular controversies. When evaluating a controversy, try to find several value conflicts, as a check on yourself.

Typical Value Conflict and Sample Controversies

Typical Value Conflict	Sample Controversies
1. Loyalty–honesty	Should you tell your parents about your sister's drug habit?
2. Competition–cooperation	Do you support the grading system?
3. Freedom of press–national security	Is it wise to hold weekly presidential press conferences?
4. Equality–individualism	Are racial quotas for employment fair?
5. Order–freedom of speech	Should we imprison those with radical ideas?
6. Rationality–spontaneity	Should you check the odds before placing a bet?

THE COMMUNICATOR'S BACKGROUND AS A CLUE TO VALUE ASSUMPTIONS

We suggested earlier that a good starting point in finding assumptions is to check the background of the author. Find out as much as you can about the value preferences usually held by a person like the writer or speaker. Is she a corporate executive, a union leader, a Republican Party official, a doctor, or a tenant in an apartment? What interests does such a person naturally wish to protect? There is certainly nothing inherently wrong with pursuing self-interest, but such pursuits often limit the value assumptions a particular writer will tolerate. For example, it is highly unlikely that the president of a major cigarette firm would place a high value on compassion for the vulnerable when a preference for compassion for the vulnerable rather than stability would lead to his losing his job. Consequently, you as a critical reader or listener can often quickly discover value preferences by thinking about the probable assumptions made by a person like the communicator.

A note of caution: It isn't necessarily true that because a person is a member of a group, she shares the particular value assumptions of the group. It would be a mistake to presume that every individual who belongs to a given group thinks identically. We all know that business people, farmers, and firefighters sometimes disagree among themselves when discussing particular controversies. Investigating the speaker or writer's background as a clue to her value assumptions is only a clue, and, like other clues, it can be misleading unless it is used with care.

CONSEQUENCES AS CLUES TO VALUE ASSUMPTIONS

In prescriptive arguments, each position with respect to an issue leads to different consequences or outcomes. Each of the potential consequences will have a certain likelihood of occurring, and each will also have some level of desirability or undesirability.

How desirable a consequence is for an argued position will depend on personal value preferences. The desirability of the conclusions in such cases will be dictated by the probability of the potential consequences and the importance attached to them. Thus, an important means of determining an individual's value assumptions is to note the reasons given in support of a conclusion and then to determine what value priorities would lead to these reasons being judged as more desirable than reasons that might have been offered on the other side of the issue. Let's take a look at a concrete example.

> Nuclear power plants should not be built because they will pollute our environment with dangerous waste material.

The reason provided here is a rather specific potential consequence of building nuclear plants. This writer clearly sees environmental pollution as very undesirable. Why does this consequence carry so much weight in this person's thinking? What more general value does preventing pollution help achieve? We are only guessing, but probably public health or conservation is being weighted especially heavily by this person. Someone else might stress a different consequence in this argument, such as the effect on the supply of electricity to consumers. Why? Probably because he values efficiency very highly! Thus, the given reason supports the conclusion if a value assumption is made that public health or conservation is more important than efficiency.

One important means of determining value assumptions, then, is to ask the question, "Why are the particular consequences or outcomes presented as reasons so desirable to the person?"

Remember: When you identify, you should always try to state value priorities. With controversial topics, stating value assumptions in this way will be a continual reminder both of what the writer is giving up and of what she is gaining. Try to resist the temptation to stop your analysis prematurely by just identifying the values of the speaker or writer. Identifying those values is a step on the way to finding the value priority assumptions, but by itself it provides very little assistance in understanding an argument. Values, by their nature, are possessed by us all.

MORE HINTS FOR FINDING VALUE ASSUMPTIONS

Another useful technique for generating value conflicts is to reverse role-play. Ask the question, "What do those people who would take a different position from a stated argument care about?" When someone argues that we should not use monkeys in experimental research, you should ask yourself, "If I wanted to defend the use of monkeys, what would I be concerned about?"

Finally, you can always check to see whether the disagreement results from a value conflict concerning the rights of an individual to behave in a particular

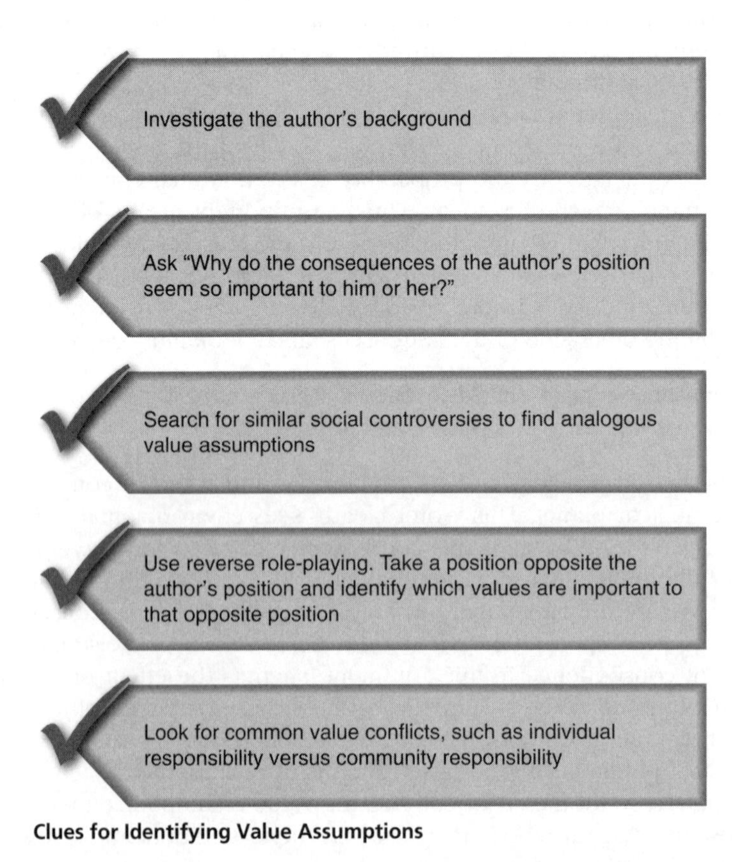

Clues for Identifying Value Assumptions

fashion and the welfare of the group affected by the behavior in question. Many arguments rest implicitly on a stance with respect to this enduring value conflict. Like other common value conflicts, we can all recall numerous instances when our thinking required us to weigh these two important values and their effects.

For example, when we wonder about the use of metal detectors in the public schools, we often begin to construct our arguments in terms of thinking about the privacy rights of the individual students and the threats to the student body if a student were to bring a weapon to school. Then, we try to balance those values against other values: Does the individual's right to privacy deserve greater protection than the welfare of the other students in the school in this instance? What other issues are involved in this value conflict? What about the request of skinheads to parade through ethnic neighborhoods?

FINDING VALUE ASSUMPTIONS ON YOUR OWN

Let's work on an example together to help you become more comfortable with finding value assumptions.

> Different workplaces have different working environments. Some offer competitive wages, where performance is evaluated and compared with that of others and they may or may not get a pay raise accordingly. Some places like to encourage an environment where everyone works together as a group. Pay raises in this environment are usually done by amount of education or experience. This type of workplace allows for workers to form good relationships and work together as a team. Which work environment would really have the best productivity? One where everyone was pitted against everyone else and productivity was the only basis for pay raises, or one where the environment fosters a team that works together to up the productivity?

The structure of the two positions is outlined here for you:

CONCLUSION 1: *The workplace should offer competitive wages.*

REASON: *The only basis for salary increases is productivity; therefore, this type of workplace creates optimal incentives for hard work.*

CONCLUSION 2: *The workplace should offer a team environment.*

REASON: *If the staff respect each other, they create an environment that can be healthy and effectively productive.*

Notice that the work environment where wages are based on individual productivity values competition. Those who organize that kind of environment believe that competition would create more productivity because it motivates the individual. Thus, they contend that a team environment would get in the way of the productivity of the competitive environment.

> VALUE ASSUMPTION: *In this context, competition is valued over cooperation.*

On the other hand, those who think the team environment would be the most productive, value cooperation. They believe that working together helps the group become motivated to be more productive, not just for themselves, but for the company (the team). They think that the group work would create a better working environment than one that offered competitive wages.

> VALUE ASSUMPTION: *In this situation, cooperation is valued over competition.*

Therefore, the major value conflict is cooperation versus competition. A supporter of the competitive wage environment believes that competition, rather than cooperation, among coworkers over pay will create the most productive environment. Her stance on this issue does not mean that she does not value cooperation; both values are probably very important to her. In the instance of the workplace, however, competition has taken over.

Remember that complete reasoning with respect to prescriptive issues requires reasons *and* value assumptions.

USING THIS CRITICAL QUESTION

Once you have found a value assumption, what do you do with it? First, recall the purpose of every critical question—to move you toward the evaluation of reasoning! Because you know that thoughtful people have different value assumptions, you have the right to wonder why any single value assumption is being made. Thus, as a critical thinker, you would want to point out the need for anyone who is making an argument to offer some explanation for why you should accept the particular value assumption that is implicit in that argument.

VALUES AND RELATIVISM

We do not want to give the impression in this chapter that value preferences are like ice cream, such that when I choose blueberry cheesecake as my flavor, you have no basis for trying to persuade me that the lemon chiffon is a better choice. Ice cream is just a matter of personal preference—end of story!

However, the choice of value preferences requires reasoning. That reasoning, like any other, can be informed, thoughtful, and caring. But it can also be sloppy and self-absorbed. Hence, value preferences require some justification that critical thinkers can consider. A value preference requires supporting reasons just as any other conclusion does. Then each of us can study the reasoning to form our own reaction.

IDENTIFYING AND EVALUATING DESCRIPTIVE ASSUMPTIONS

When you find value assumptions, you know pretty well what a writer or speaker wants the world to be like—what goals she thinks are most important. But you do not know what she takes for granted about the nature of the world and the people who inhabit it. For example, are people basically lazy or achievement oriented, cooperative or competitive, controlled by their biological makeup or by their environment, self-interested or altruistic, rational or whimsical? Her visible reasoning depends on ideas like these, as well as upon her values. Such unstated ideas are descriptive assumptions, and they too are essential hidden elements of an argument.

The following argument about a car depends on hidden assumptions. Can you find them?

> This car will get you to your destination, whatever it may be. I have driven this model of car on multiple occasions.

Critical Question: ***What are the descriptive assumptions?***

Descriptive assumptions are beliefs about the way the world *was, is, or will be*; prescriptive or value assumptions, you remember, are beliefs about how the world *should be.*

ILLUSTRATING DESCRIPTIVE ASSUMPTIONS

Let's examine our argument about the car to illustrate more clearly what we mean by a descriptive assumption.

The reasoning structure is:

CONCLUSION: *This particular car will get you where you want to go.*

REASON: *This model of car has functioned well on multiple occasions.*

The reasoning thus far is incomplete. We know that, by itself, a reason just does not have a direct link to a conclusion; the reason must be connected to the conclusion by certain other (frequently unstated) ideas. These ideas, if true, justify treating the reason as support for the conclusion. Thus, whether a reason supports, or is relevant to, a conclusion depends on whether we can locate unstated ideas that logically connect the reason to the conclusion. When such unstated ideas are descriptive, we call them descriptive assumptions. Let us present two such assumptions for the above argument.

ASSUMPTION 1: *From year to year, a particular model of car has a consistent quality.*

First, no such statement was provided in the argument itself. However, if the reason is true and if this assumption is true, then the reason provides some support for the conclusion. But if not all model years have the same level of dependability (and we know they do not), then experience with a model in previous years cannot be a reliable guide to whether one should buy the car in the current model year. Note that this assumption is a statement about the way things *are*, not about the way things *should be*. Thus, it is a descriptive connecting assumption.

> ASSUMPTION 2: *The driving that would be done with the new car is the same kind of driving that was done by the person recommending the car.*

When we speak about "driving" a car, the ambiguity of driving can get us into trouble if we do not clarify the term. If the "driving" of the person recommending the car refers to regular trips to the grocery store on a quiet suburban street with no hills, that driving experience is not very relevant as a comparator when the new car is to be driven in Colorado, while pulling a heavy trailer. Thus, this conclusion is supported by the reason only if a certain definition of driving is assumed.

We can call this kind of descriptive assumption a *definitional assumption* because we have taken for granted one meaning of a term that could have more than one meaning. Thus, one very important kind of descriptive assumption to look for is a definitional assumption—the taking for granted of one meaning for a term that has multiple possible meanings.

Once you have identified the connecting assumptions, you have answered the question, "On what basis can that conclusion be drawn from that reason?" The next natural step is to ask, "Is there any basis for accepting the assumptions?" If not, then, for you, the reason fails to provide support for the conclusion. If so, then the reason provides logical support for the conclusion. Thus, you can say reasoning is sound when you have identified connecting assumptions and you have good reason to believe those assumptions.

***Attention:* A descriptive assumption is an unstated belief about how the world was, is, or will become.**

When you identify assumptions, you identify ideas the communicator needs to take for granted so that the reason is supportive of the conclusion. Because writers and speakers frequently are not aware of their own assumptions, their conscious beliefs may be quite different from the ideas you identify as implicit assumptions.

CLUES FOR LOCATING ASSUMPTIONS

Your task in finding assumptions is to reconstruct the reasoning by filling in the missing links. You want to provide ideas that help the communicator's reasoning "make sense." Once you have a picture of the entire argument, both the visible and the invisible elements, you will be in a much better position to determine its strengths and weaknesses.

How does one go about finding these important missing links? It requires hard work, imagination, and creativity. Finding important assumptions is a difficult task. Earlier in this chapter, we gave you several hints for finding value assumptions. Here are some clues that will make your search for descriptive assumptions successful.

Keep thinking about the gap between the conclusion and reasons. Why are you looking for assumptions in thc first place? You are looking because you want to be able to judge how well the reasons support the conclusions. Thus, look for what the writer or speaker would have had to take for granted to link the reasons with the conclusion. Keep asking, "How do you get from the reason to the conclusion?" Ask, "If the reason is true, what else must be true for the conclusion to follow?" And, to help answer that question, you will find it very helpful to ask, "Supposing the reason(s) were true, is there any way in which the conclusion nevertheless could be false?"

Searching for the gap will be helpful for finding both value and descriptive assumptions.

Look for unstated ideas that support reasons. Sometimes a reason is presented with no explicit support; yet the plausibility of the reason depends on the acceptability of ideas that have been taken for granted. These ideas are descriptive assumptions. The following outline of a brief argument illustrates such a case:

CONCLUSION: *All high school English class students will go see at least one Shakespeare play.*

REASON: *It is beneficial to experience Shakespeare's works firsthand.*

What ideas must be taken for granted for this reason to be acceptable? We must assume:

a. The performance will be well done and reflective of what Shakespeare would encourage, and

b. students will understand the play and be able to relate it to Shakespeare.

Both (a) and (b) are ideas that have to be taken for granted for the reason to be acceptable and, thus, potentially supportive of the conclusion.

Identify with the writer or speaker. Locating someone's assumptions is often made easier by imagining that you were asked to defend the conclusion. If you can, crawl into the skin of a person who would reach such a conclusion. Discover his background. When an executive for a coal company argues that strip mining does not significantly harm the beauty of our natural environment, he has probably begun with a belief that strip mining is beneficial to our nation. Thus, he may assume a definition of beauty that would be consistent with his arguments, while other definitions of beauty would lead to a condemnation of strip mining.

Identify with the opposition. If you are unable to locate assumptions by taking the role of the speaker or writer, try to reverse roles. Ask yourself why anyone might disagree with the conclusion. What type of reasoning would prompt someone to disagree with the conclusion you are evaluating? If you can play the role of a person who would not accept the conclusion, you can more readily see assumptions imbedded in the explicit structure of the argument.

Recognize the potential existence of other means of attaining the advantages referred to in the reasons. Frequently, a conclusion is supported by reasons that indicate the various advantages of acting on the author's conclusion. When there are many ways to reach the same advantages, one important assumption linking the reasons to the conclusion is that the best way to attain the advantages is through the one advocated by the communicator.

Let's try this technique with one brief example. Experts disagree about how a person should establish financial stability. Often, young people are encouraged to establish financial stability with a credit card. But aren't there many ways to establish financial stability? Might not some of these alternatives have less serious disadvantages than those that could result when a young person spends too much on that credit card? For example, investing some money in a savings account or establishing credit by maintaining a checking account are viable routes to establishing financial stability. Thus, those who suggest that people get credit cards to help establish financial stability are not taking into account the risks involved with their solution or the possibility of an alternative with fewer risks.

Avoid stating incompletely established reasons as assumptions. When you first attempt to locate descriptive assumptions, you may find yourself locating a stated reason, thinking that the reason has not been adequately established, and asserting, "That's only an assumption. You don't know that to be the case." Or you might simply restate the reason as the assumption. You may have correctly identified a need on the part of the writer or speaker to better establish the truth of her reason. While this clarification is an important insight on your part, you have not identified an assumption in the sense that we have been using it in this chapter. You are simply labeling a reason "an assumption."

Do you see that when you do this, all you are doing is stating that the author's reason is her assumption—when what you are probably really trying to stress is that the author's reason has not been sufficiently established by evidence.

AVOIDING ANALYSIS OF TRIVIAL ASSUMPTIONS

We make certain assumptions about communicators that we take for granted and thus do not need to evaluate. You will want to devote your energy to evaluating important assumptions, so we want to warn you about some potential trivial assumptions. By trivial, we mean a descriptive assumption that is self-evident.

You, as a reader or listener, can assume that the communicator believes his reasons are true. You may want to attack the reasons as insufficient, but it is trivial to point out the writer's or speaker's assumption that the reasons are true.

Another type of trivial assumption concerns the reasoning structure. You may be tempted to state that the writer believes that the reason and conclusion are logically related. Right—but trivial. What is important is how they are logically related. It is also trivial to point out that an argument assumes that we can understand the logic, that we can understand the terminology, or that we have the appropriate background knowledge.

Avoid spending time on analyzing trivial assumptions. Your search for assumptions will be most rewarding when you locate hidden, debatable missing links.

ASSUMPTIONS AND YOUR OWN WRITING AND SPEAKING

At this point in the chapter, you may be tempted to conclude that your goal as a writer is to avoid incorporating your value preferences and descriptive beliefs in your writing. Because we have discussed the danger of unstated assumptions to critical evaluation, you may wonder whether we expect you to set aside your beliefs and stick to the facts.

Before we continue down this line of thinking, let's consider that statement. "Stick to the facts." Which facts? How will you decide which facts are most powerful to you? How will you decide which facts to exclude? How will you interpret facts and draw conclusions about them? What will you consider to be the implications of these facts? Sticking to the facts is easier said than done.

Consider this fact: More than half of athletic departments in the highest level of intercollegiate athletics are subsidized by their states, student fees, and the university. Does this information bother you? Seems perfectly acceptable? Should we explore remedies or do we consider this cost reasonable considering the benefits students and citizens receive by having a successful football team? Your response to this fact is influenced by your value preferences and descriptive beliefs about the purpose of the university and the importance of team sports in our culture.

This example illustrates an important point: You will never be able to write without your values and descriptive beliefs influencing your arguments. Forgetting about your assumptions is hardly the goal of effective writing and speaking. We are human beings, not computer programs. We have developed these deeply engrained beliefs because of our lives and experiences. These beliefs influence the way we see the world in important ways.

If values and descriptive beliefs are an important and inevitable part of writing and thinking, what's the big deal? Why did we devote an entire chapter of a critical thinking text to the subject? Writers should be particularly concerned about the influence of these beliefs in their writing for two reasons. First, these beliefs are often unstated or assumed. As such, readers usually miss them entirely. They may not even know that they ought to keep an eye out for them. The author usually does not provide a defense or an explanation for why he holds the belief. The author probably isn't being sneaky, slipping an unstated assumption into an argument. The author, instead, is probably unaware that he assumes that collective responsibility trumps individual responsibility or that the quality of public education is more important than lower taxes. He may just assume that these beliefs are actually self-evident truths that we all agree on. When you write, try as best you can to reveal the assumptions that are guiding your thoughts. Give those who are receiving your communication attempts a fair chance to fully understand the basis for your reasoning. Share with them why you are so convinced that these assumptions are correct .

Clues for Discovering Descriptive Assumptions

1. Keep thinking about the gap between the conclusion and reasons.
2. Look for ideas that support reasons.
3. Identify with the opposition.
4. Recognize the potential existence of other means of attaining the advantages referred to in the reasons.
5. Learn more about the issues.

PRACTICE EXERCISES

Critical Question: ***What are the value and descriptive assumptions?***

For each of the three passages, locate important assumptions made by the author. Remember first to determine the conclusion and the reasons.

Passage 1

Sometimes, it is not best to be completely honest. Some personal beliefs are better left unsaid. For instance, if you are talking to a friend and he asks for your opinion about something, the truth should be avoided if there is no way to deliver it without harming the relationship.

The truth is not always necessary. If you were a doctor and you had to give your patient bad news about his health, then it is important to maintain honesty. However, sometimes, in the case of friendship, honesty may need some buffering.

Passage 2

College sororities and fraternities get a bad rap for their hazing and partying, but joining such organizations has many benefits that should make you seriously consider pledging them. For example, a big benefit is the bonding with true brothers and sisters that occurs, making you friends for life. A related benefit is networking. When seeking a job after graduation, most of you will find your future prospects not from what you know, but whom you know. By joining a fraternity or sorority, you gain access to a vast network of working professionals. Another major benefit is the ability to take part in leadership roles that give you the skills to compete in the working world, since fraternities and sororities are always organizing events like dinners and parties. Lastly, joining a sorority or fraternity gives you a great opportunity to have lots of fun while socializing and becoming close friends with numerous people. Your college years should be much more than going to class and studying; they should be among the best years of your life.

Passage 3

Adopted children should have the right to find out who their biological parents are. They should be able to find their biological parents for personal and health reasons. Most children would want to know what happened to these people and why they were given up for adoption. Even though this meeting may not be completely the way the child had imagined it, this interaction could provide a real sense of closure for adopted children.

Sample Responses

In presenting assumptions for the following arguments, we will list only some of the assumptions being made—those which we believe are among the most significant.

Passage 1

CONCLUSION: *Lying to spare someone's feelings is appropriate in certain situations.*

REASON: *Telling the truth could harm a friendship.*

The reason stresses the negative consequence of harming a relationship. Thus, one value conflict that relates to this argument is that between honesty and harmony. Of course, others would argue that honesty is the best foundation for the kind of friendship they seek. A value preference for harmony over honesty links the reason to the conclusion.

As with most prescriptive controversies, more than one value conflict is involved in this dilemma. For example, this controversy also requires us to think about comfort over courage.

Passage 2

CONCLUSION: *College students should consider joining a fraternity or sorority.*

REASONS:

1. *Students develop strong bonds with others.*
2. *The interaction with others promotes networking helpful for getting jobs.*
3. *Sororities and fraternity activities facilitate leadership skills.*
4. *Fraternities and sororities promote socializing and having a lot of fun.*

What links these reasons to the conclusion? Can they be true, yet *not* support the conclusion? Value priorities are a needed link. An assumed value priority that a sense of belonging and fun are more important than self-discipline and academic excellence links the reasons to the conclusion. A debatable descriptive assumption also links the reasons to the conclusion: Benefits of a sorority cannot be acquired through other choices such as on-campus clubs and organizations. Are there any ideas taken for granted that are necessary for us to accept the truth of any of the reasons? The first reason will be true only if potential employers see a history of belonging to a fraternity or sorority as a plus on one's resume. It is possible, for example, that many employers will view this background as a sign of lack of independence, seriousness, and drive.

CHAPTER

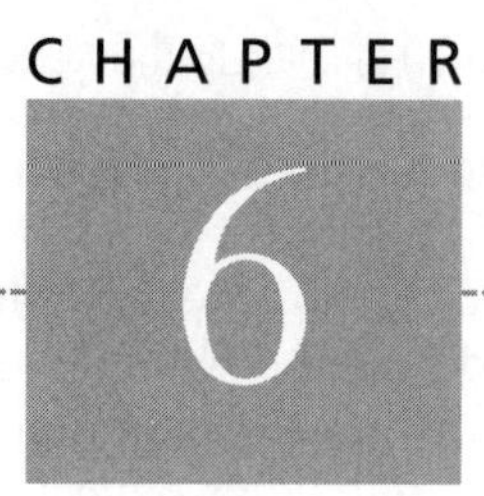

Are There Any Fallacies in the Reasoning?

Thus far, you have been working at taking the raw materials a writer or speaker gives you and assembling them into a meaningful overall structure. You have learned ways to remove the irrelevant parts from your pan as well as how to discover the "invisible glue" that holds the relevant parts together—that is, the assumptions. All these things have been achieved by asking critical questions. Let's briefly review these questions:

1. What are the issue and the conclusion?
2. What are the reasons?
3. What words or phrases are ambiguous?
4. What are the value and descriptive assumptions?

Asking these questions should give you a clear understanding of the communicator's reasoning as well as a sense of where there might be strengths and weaknesses in the argument. Most remaining chapters focus on how well the structure holds up after being assembled. Your major question now is, "How acceptable is the conclusion in light of the reasons provided?" You are now ready to make your central focus evaluation. Remember: The objective of critical reading and listening is to judge the acceptability or worth of conclusions.

Answering our first four questions has been a necessary beginning to the evaluation process; we now move to questions requiring us to make judgments more directly and explicitly about the worth or the quality of the reasoning. Our task now is to separate the fool's gold from the genuine gold. We want to isolate the best reasons—those that we want to treat most seriously.

Your first step at this stage of the evaluation process is to examine the reasoning structure to determine whether the communicator's reasoning has depended on false or highly doubtful assumptions or has "tricked" you through either a mistake in logic or other forms of deceptive reasoning. Chapter 5 focused on finding and then thinking about the quality of assumptions. This chapter, on the other hand, highlights those reasoning "tricks" called *fallacies*.

Three common tricks are:

1. providing reasoning that requires *erroneous or incorrect assumptions*, thus making it irrelevant to the conclusion;
2. *distracting us* by making information seem relevant to the conclusion when it is not; and
3. providing support for the conclusion that depends on the conclusion already being true.

Spotting such tricks will prevent us from being unduly influenced by them. Let's see what a fallacy in reasoning looks like.

> Dear Editor: I was shocked by your paper's support of Senator Spendall's arguments for a tax hike to increase state money available for improving highways. Of course the Senator favors such a hike. What else would you expect from a tax and spend liberal.

Note that the letter at first appears to be presenting a "reason" to dispute the tax hike proposal, by citing the senator's liberal reputation. But the reason is *not relevant* to the conclusion. The question is whether the tax hike is a good idea. The letter writer has ignored the senator's reasons and has provided no specific reasons against the tax hike; instead, she has personally attacked the senator by labeling him a "tax and spend liberal." The writer has committed a fallacy in reasoning, because her argument requires an absurd assumption to be relevant to the conclusion and shifts attention from the argument to the arguer—Senator Spendall. An unsuspecting reader not alert to this fallacy may be tricked into thinking that the writer has provided a persuasive reason.

This chapter gives you practice in identifying such fallacies so that you will not fall for such tricks.

Critical Question: ***Are there any fallacies in the reasoning?***

Attention: *A fallacy is a reasoning "trick" that an author might use while trying to persuade you to accept a conclusion.*

A QUESTIONING APPROACH TO FINDING REASONING FALLACIES

There are numerous reasoning fallacies. And they can be organized in many different ways. Many are so common that they have been given formal names. You can find many lengthy lists of fallacies in numerous texts and Web sites. Fortunately, you don't need to be aware of all the fallacies and their names to be able to locate them. If you ask yourself the right questions, you will be able to find reasoning fallacies—even if you cannot name them.

Thus, we have adopted the strategy of emphasizing self-questioning strategies, rather than asking you to memorize an extensive list of possible kinds of fallacies. We believe, however, that knowing the names of the most common fallacies can sensitize you to fallacies and also act as a language shortcut in communicating your reaction to faulty reasoning to others familiar with the names. Thus, we provide you with the names of fallacies as we identify the deceptive reasoning processes and encourage you to learn the names of the common fallacies described on page 86 at the end of the chapter.

We have already introduced one common fallacy to you in our *letter to the editor* example mentioned earlier. We noted that the writer personally attacked Senator Spendall instead of responding directly to the senator's reasons. The reasoning illustrates the *ad hominem fallacy*. The Latin phrase *ad hominem* means "against the man or against the person." Ad hominem is considered a fallacy because the character or interests of individuals making arguments are usually not relevant to the quality of the argument being made. It is attacking the messenger instead of addressing the message.

Here is another brief example of ad hominem reasoning.

Sandy: "I believe that joining sororities is a waste of time and money."

Julie: "Of course you would say that, you didn't get accepted by any sorority."

Sandy: "But what about the arguments I gave to support my position?"

Julie: "Those don't count. You're just a sore loser."

You can start your list of fallacy names with this one. Here is the definition:

Fallacy: Ad Hominem: An attack, or an insult, on the person, rather than directly addressing the person's reasons.

EVALUATING ASSUMPTIONS AS A STARTING POINT

If you have been able to locate assumptions (see Chapter 5), especially descriptive assumptions, you already possess a major skill in determining questionable assumptions and in finding fallacies. The more questionable the assumption is, the less relevant the reasoning will be. Some "reasons," such as ad hominem arguments, will be so irrelevant to the conclusion that you would have to supply blatantly erroneous assumptions to provide a logical link. Such reasoning is a fallacy, and you should immediately reject it.

In the next section, we take you through some exercises in discovering other common fallacies. Once you know how to look, you will be able to find most fallacies. We suggest that you adopt the following thinking steps in locating fallacies:

To demonstrate the process you should go through to evaluate assumptions and thus recognize many fallacies, we will examine the quality of the reasoning in the following passage. We will begin by assembling the structure.

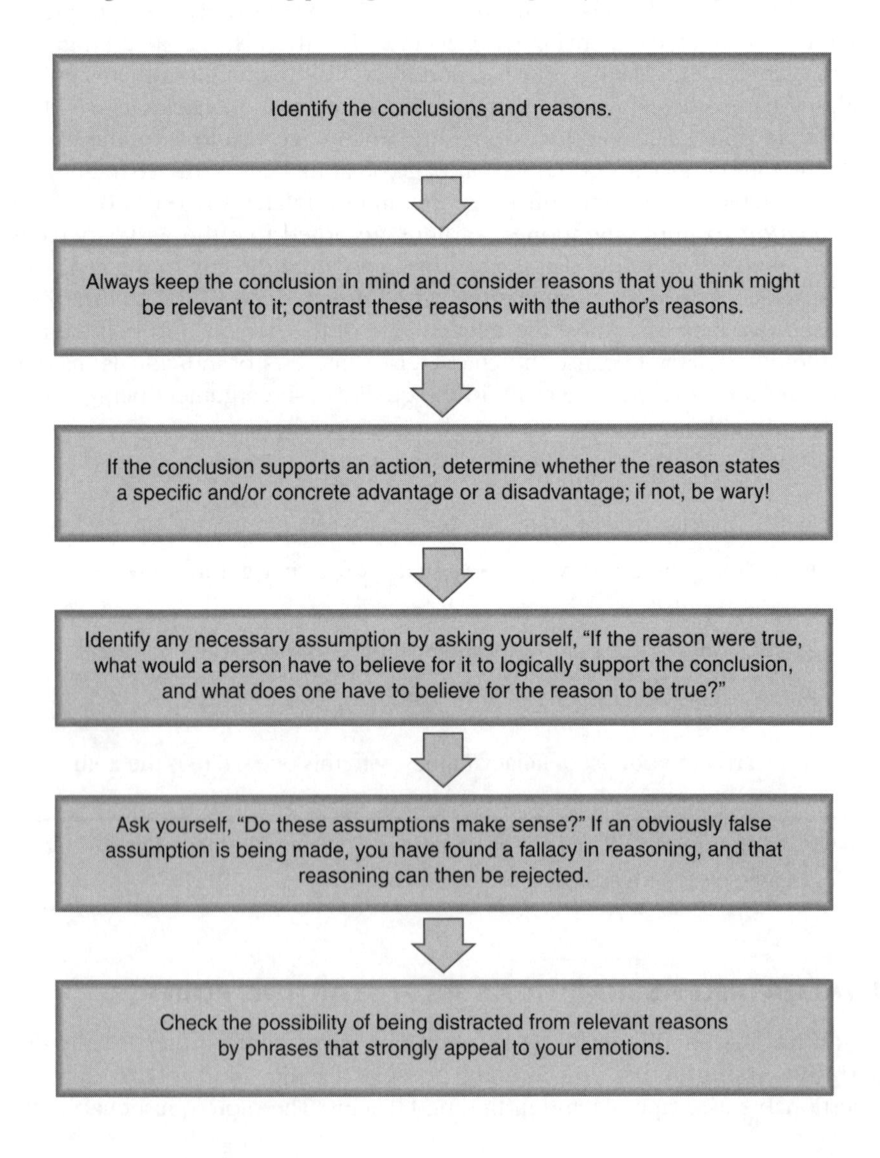

The question involved in this legislation is not really a question of whether alcohol consumption is or is not detrimental to health. Rather, it is a question of whether Congress is willing to have the Federal Communications Commission make an arbitrary decision that prohibits alcohol advertising on radio and television. If we should permit the FCC to take this action in regard to alcohol, what is there to prevent it from deciding next year that candy is detrimental to public health in that it causes obesity, tooth decay, and other health problems? What about milk and eggs? Milk and eggs are high in saturated animal fat and no doubt increase the cholesterol in the bloodstream, believed by many heart specialists to be a contributing factor in heart disease. Do we want the FCC to be able to prohibit the advertising of milk, eggs, butter, and ice cream on TV?

Also, we all know that no action by the federal government, however drastic, can or will be effective in eliminating alcohol consumption completely. If people want to drink alcoholic beverages, they will find some way to do so.

CONCLUSION: *The FCC should not prohibit alcohol advertising on radio and television.*

REASONS:
1. *If we permit the FCC to prohibit advertising on radio and television, the FCC will soon prohibit many kinds of advertising, because many products present potential health hazards.*
2. *No action by the federal government can or will be effective in eliminating alcohol consumption completely.*

First, we should note that both reasons refer to rather specific disadvantages of the prohibition—a good start. The acceptability of the first reason, however, depends on a hidden assumption that once we allow actions to be taken on the merits of one case, it will be impossible to stop actions on similar cases. We do not agree with this assumption because we believe that there are plenty of steps in our legal system to prevent such actions if they appear unjustified. Thus, we judge this reason to be unacceptable. Such reasoning is an example of the *slippery slope fallacy*.

Fallacy: Slippery Slope: Making the assumption that a proposed step will set off an uncontrollable chain of undesirable events, when procedures exist to prevent such a chain of events.

The relevance of the second reason is questionable because even if this reason were true, the assumption linking the reason to the conclusion—the major goal of prohibiting alcohol advertising on radio and television is to *eliminate alcohol consumption completely*—is false. A more likely goal is to *reduce consumption*. Thus we reject this reason. We call this fallacy the *searching for perfect solutions fallacy*. It takes the following form: A solution to X does not deserve our support unless it destroys the problem entirely. If we ever find a perfect solution, then we should adopt it. But the fact that part of a problem remains after a solution is tried does not mean the solution is unwise. A particular solution may be vastly superior to no solution at all. It may move us closer to solving the problem completely.

If we wait for perfect solutions to emerge, we would often find ourselves paralyzed, unable to act. Here is another example of this fallacy: It's a waste of money to add a security system to your home. If thieves want to break into your house, they will find a way to do so, regardless of any security system.

Fallacy: Searching for Perfect Solution: Falsely assuming that because part of a problem remains after a solution is tried, the solution should not be adopted.

DISCOVERING OTHER COMMON REASONING FALLACIES

We are now going to take you through some exercises in discovering more common fallacies. As you encounter each exercise, try to apply the fallacy, finding hints that we listed earlier. Once you have developed good fallacy-detection habits, you will be able to find most fallacies. Each exercise presents some reasoning that includes fallacies. We indicate why we believe the reasoning is fallacious and then name and define the fallacy.

Exercise A

It's about time that we make marijuana an option for people in chronic severe pain. We approve drugs when society reaches a consensus about their value, and there is clearly now a consensus for such approval. A recent survey of public opinion reported that 73 percent thought medical marijuana should be allowed. In addition, the California Association for the Treatment of AIDS Victims supports smoking marijuana as a treatment option for AIDS patients.

As a first step in analyzing for fallacies, let's outline the argument.

CONCLUSION: *Smoking marijuana should be a medical option.*

REASONS:
1. *We approve drugs when a consensus of their medical value has been reached, and a recent survey shows a consensus approving marijuana as a medical treatment.*
2. *A California association supports medical marijuana use.*

First, we should note that neither reason points out a specific advantage of medical marijuana; thus we should be wary from the start. Next, a close look at the wording in the first reason shows a shift in meaning of a key term, and this shift tricks us. The meaning of the word *consensus* shifts in such a way that it looks like the communicator has made a relevant argument when she has not. Consensus for drug approval usually means the consensus of scientific researchers about its merits, which is a very different consensus than the agreement of the American public on an opinion poll. Thus the reason fails to make sense, and we should reject it.

We call this mistake in reasoning the *equivocation fallacy*. Whenever you see a key word or phrase in an argument used more than once, check to see that the meaning has not changed; if it has, be alert to the equivocation fallacy. Highly ambiguous terms or phrases are especially good candidates for the equivocation fallacy.

See whether you can detect the equivocation in the following disagreement:

Ronda: Curtis is not a real man. He looked scared to death when that drunk at the bar threatened to punch him.

Ellen: If he's not a real man, how do you account for those incredibly bulging biceps?

Fallacy: Equivocation: A key word or phrase is used with two or more meanings in an argument such that the argument fails to make sense once the shifts in meaning are recognized.

Well, even if there is tricky use of the word *consensus*, in the medical marijuana argument, don't the survey results by themselves still support the conclusion? They do, *only if* we accept the assumption that when some idea is popular, then it must be good—a mistaken assumption. The public often has not sufficiently studied a problem to provide a reasoned judgment. Be wary of appeals to common opinion or to popular sentiment. We label this mistake in reasoning the *appeal to popularity fallacy*.

Fallacy: Appeal to Popularity (Ad Populum): An attempt to justify a claim by appealing to sentiments that large groups of people have in common; falsely assumes that anything favored by a large group is desirable.

Now, carefully examine the author's second reason. What assumption is being made? To prove that medical marijuana is desirable, she *appeals to questionable authorities*—a California association. A position is not good just because the authorities are for it. What is important in determining the relevance of such reasoning is the evidence that the authorities are using in making their judgment. Unless we know that these authorities have special knowledge about this issue, we must treat this reason as a fallacy. Such a fallacy is called the *appeal to questionable authority fallacy.*

Fallacy: Appeal to Questionable Authority: Supporting a conclusion by citing an authority who lacks special expertise on the issue at hand.

Now let's examine some arguments related to another controversy: Should Congress approve a federally funded child development program that would provide day-care centers for children?

Exercise B

I am against the government's child development program. First, I am interested in protecting the children of this country. They need to be protected from social planners and self-righteous ideologues who would disrupt the normal course of children's lives and tear them from their mothers and families to make them pawns in a universal scheme designed to produce infinite happiness in 20 years. Children should grow up with their mothers, not with a series of caretakers and nurses' aides. What is at issue is whether parents shall continue to have the right to form the characters of their children, or whether the state with all its power should be given the tools and techniques for forming the young.

Let's again begin by outlining the argument.

CONCLUSION: *The government's child development program is a mistake.*

REASONS:
1. *Our children need to be protected from social planners and self-righteous ideologues, who would disrupt the normal course of children's lives and tear them from their families.*
2. *The parents, not the state, should have the right to form the characters of their children.*

As critical thinkers, we should be looking for specific facts about the program. But we find none. The reason is saturated with undefined and emotionally loaded generalities. We have italicized several of these terms in the passage. Such terms will typically generate negative emotions, which the writer or speaker hopes readers and listeners will associate with the position she is attacking.

The writer plays two common tricks on us. First, she is *appealing to our emotions* with her choice of words, hoping that our emotional reactions will get us to agree with her conclusion. When communicators stimulate emotional reactions from people and then use that reaction to get them to agree to their conclusion, they commit the fallacy of an *appeal to emotion.* This fallacy occurs when such emotional reactions should not be relevant to the truth or falsity of a conclusion. Three especially common places for finding this fallacy are advertising, political debate, and the courtroom. A common form of this fallacy is *name-calling*, a form of ad hominem, which is an attempt to discredit individuals by labeling them with words that have unfavorable emotional associations. The phrase "self-righteous ideologues" illustrates name-calling.

Fallacy: Appeals to Emotions: The use of emotionally charged language to distract readers and listeners from relevant reasons and evidence. Common emotions appealed to are fear, hope, patriotism, pity, and sympathy.

Second, the writer has set up a position to attack, which in fact does not exist, making it much easier to get us on her side. She has extended the opposition's position to an "easy-to-attack" position. The false assumption in this case is that the position attacked is the same as the position actually presented in the legislation. Will children really be pawns in some universal scheme? The lesson for the critical thinker is: When someone attacks aspects of a position, always check to see whether she is fairly representing the position. If she is not, you have located the *straw-person fallacy.*

A straw person is not real and is easy to knock down—as is the position attacked when someone commits the straw-person fallacy. The best way to check how fairly a position is being represented is to get the facts about all positions.

Fallacy: Straw Person: Distorting our opponent's point of view so that it is easy to attack; thus we attack a point of view that does not truly exist.

Let's now look closely at the second reason. The writer states that either parents have the right to form the characters of their children or the state should be given the decisive tools. Take a quick look at another example in a statement by Britney Spears in *Circus:* "There are only two types of people in the world: the ones that entertain and the ones that observe."

For statements like these to be true, one must assume that there are only two choices. Are there? No! The writer has created a *false dilemma.* Isn't it possible for the child development program to exist and also for the family to have a significant influence on the child? Always be cautious when controversies are treated as if only two choices are possible; there are usually more than two. When a communicator oversimplifies an issue by stating only two choices, the error is referred to as an *either-or* or *false dilemma* fallacy. To find *either-or* fallacies, be on the alert for phrases like the following:

either . . . or

the only alternative is

the two choices are

because A has not worked, only B will.

Seeing these phrases does not necessarily mean that you have located a fallacy. Sometimes there *are* only two options. These phrases are just caution signs causing you to pause and wonder: "Are there more than two options in this case?"

Can you see the false dilemma in the following interchange?

> Citizen: I think that the decision by the United States to invade Iraq was a big mistake.
>
> Politician: Why do you hate America?

Fallacy: Either-Or (or False Dilemma): Assuming only two alternatives when there are more than two.

We often encounter further confusion in our thinking when we seek explanations for behavior. A brief conversation between college roommates illustrates the confusion.

> Dan: I've noticed that Chuck has been acting really weird lately. He's acting really rude toward others and is making all kinds of messes in our residence hall and refusing to clean them up. What do you think is going on?
>
> Kevin: That doesn't surprise me. He is just a jerk.

To explain requires an analysis of why a behavior occurred. Explaining is a demanding work that often tests the boundaries of what we know. In the given example, "jerkhood" is an unsatisfactory explanation of Chuck's behavior. When asked to explain why a certain behavior has occurred, it is frequently tempting to hide our ignorance of a complex sequence of causes by labeling or naming the behavior. Then we falsely assume that because we know the name, we know the cause.

We do so because the naming tricks us into believing we have identified something the person *has* or *is* that makes her act accordingly. For example, instead of specifying the complex set of internal and external factors that lead a person to express an angry emotion, such as problems with relationships, parental reinforcement practices, feelings of helplessness, lack of sleep, and life stressors, we say that the person *has* a bad temper or that the person *is* hostile. Such explanations oversimplify and prevent us from seeking more insightful understanding.

The following examples should heighten your alertness to this fallacy:

1. In response to dad's heavy drinking, mom is asked by her adult daughter, "Why is dad behaving so strangely?" Mom replies, "He's having a midlife crisis."
2. A friend worries constantly that other people are talking about him. You ask a psychologist why he does so. He answers, "Because he is paranoid."

Neither respondent satisfactorily explained what happened. For instance, the specifics of dad's genes, job pressures, marital strife, and exercise habits could have provided the basis for explaining the heavy drinking. "A midlife crisis" is not only inadequate but also misleading. We think we know why dad is drinking heavily, but we don't.

Be alert for the fallacy of explaining by naming when people claim that they have discovered a cause for the behavior when all they have actually done is named it.

Fallacy: Explaining by Naming: Falsely assuming that because you have provided a name for some event or behavior, you have also adequately explained the event.

LOOKING FOR DIVERSIONS

Frequently, those trying to get an audience to accept some claim find that they can defend that claim by preventing the audience from taking too close a look at the relevant reasons. They prevent the close look by diversion tactics. As you look for fallacies, you will find it helpful to be especially alert to reasoning used by the communicator that *diverts your attention* from the most relevant reasons. For example, the ad hominem fallacy can fool us by diverting our attention too much to the nature of the person and too little to the legitimate reasons. In this section, we present exercises that illustrate other fallacies that we are likely to detect if we ask the question, "Has the author tricked us by diverting our attention?"

Exercise C

Political speech: In the upcoming election, you have the opportunity to vote for a woman who represents the future of this great nation, who has fought for democracy and defended our flag, and who has been decisive, confident, and courageous in pursuing the American Dream. This is a caring woman who has supported our children and the environment and has helped move this country toward peace, prosperity, and freedom. A vote for Goodheart is a vote for truth, vision, and common sense.

Sounds like Ms. Goodheart is a wonderful person, doesn't it? But the speech fails to provide any specifics about the senator's past record or present position on issues. Instead, it presents a series of *virtue words* that tend to be associated with deep-seated positive emotions. We call these virtue words *glittering generalities* because they have such positive associations and are so general as to mean whatever the reader wants them to mean. The glittering generality device leads us to approve or accept a conclusion without examining relevant reasons, evidence, or specific advantages or disadvantages. The glittering generality is much like name-calling in reverse because name-calling seeks to make us form a negative judgment without examining the evidence. The use of virtue words is a popular ploy of politicians because it serves to distract the reader or listener from specific actions or policies, which can more easily trigger disagreement.

Fallacy: Glittering Generality: The use of vague, emotionally appealing virtue words that dispose us to approve something without closely examining the reasons.

Let's examine another very common diversionary device.

Exercise D

I don't understand why everyone is so upset about drug companies distorting research data in order to make their painkiller drugs seem to be less dangerous to people's health than they actually are. Taking those drugs can't be that bad. After all, there are still thousands of people using these drugs and getting pain relief from them.

What is the real issue? Is the public being misled about the safety of painkiller drugs? But if the reader is not careful, his attention will be diverted to the issue of whether the public wants to use these drugs. When a writer or speaker shifts our attention from the issue, we can say that she has drawn a *red herring* across the trail of the original issue. Many of us are adept at committing the red herring fallacy, as the following dialogue illustrates.

Mother: Why did you lie to me about where you were going with your boyfriend?

Daughter: You're always picking on me.

If the daughter is successful, the issue will become whether the mother is picking on her daughter, not why the daughter lied to her.

You should normally have no difficulty spotting red herrings as long as you keep the real issue in mind as well as the kind of evidence needed to resolve it.

Fallacy: Red Herring: An irrelevant topic is presented to divert attention from the original issue and help to win an argument by shifting attention away from the argument and to another issue. The fallacy sequence in this instance is as follows: (a) Topic A is being discussed; (b) Topic B is introduced as though it is relevant to topic A, but it is not; and (c) Topic A is abandoned.

This sort of "reasoning" is fallacious because merely changing the topic of discussion hardly counts as an argument against a claim.

SLEIGHT OF HAND: BEGGING THE QUESTION

Our last illustrated fallacy is a particularly deceptive one. Sometimes, a conclusion is supported by itself; only the words have been changed to fool the innocent! For example, to argue that dropping out of school is *undesirable* because it is *bad* is to not argue at all. The conclusion is "proven" by the same conclusion (in different words). Such an argument *begs the question*, rather than answering it. Let's look at an example that is a little less obvious.

> Reading traditional textbooks is superior to reading E-texts in learning effectiveness because it is highly advantageous for learning to have materials made available in a textbook format.

Again, the reason supporting the conclusion restates the conclusion in different words. By definition, traditional books are read in a textbook format. The writer is arguing that such a procedure is good because it is good. A legitimate reason would be one that points out a specific advantage to reading traditional textbooks such as greater retention of learned material.

Whenever a conclusion is *assumed* in the reasoning when it should have been proven, begging the question has occurred. When you outline the structure of an argument, check the reasons to be sure that they do not simply repeat the conclusion in different words and check to see that the conclusion is not used to prove the reasons. In case you are confused, let's illustrate with two examples, one argument that begs the question and one that does not.

> **(1)** To allow the press to keep their sources confidential is very advantageous to the country because it increases the likelihood that individuals will report evidence against powerful people.
> **(2)** To allow the press to keep their sources confidential is very advantageous to the country because it is highly conducive to the interests of the larger community that private individuals should have the privilege of providing information to the press without being identified.

Paragraph (2) begs the question by basically repeating the conclusion. It fails to point out what the specific advantages are and simply repeats that confidentiality of sources is socially useful.

Fallacy: Begging the Question: An argument in which the conclusion is assumed in the reasoning.

USING THIS CRITICAL QUESTION

When you spot a fallacy, you have found a legitimate basis for rejecting that part of the communicator's argument. But in the spirit of constructive critical thinking, you want to consider any reasons offered that are not fallacies. Unfortunately, the author of a book or article is unavailable for more conversation. But for those fallacies occurring in an oral argument, your best bet for an enduring conversation is to ask the person who committed the fallacy if there are any better reasons for the conclusion. For example, if a red herring fallacy occurs, ask the speaker if he could return to the original issue.

Online help: For more ideas about how to respond effectively to reasoning fallacies that occur in interpersonal situations, see http://www.pearsonhighered.com/browne, Chapter 6.

SUMMARY OF REASONING ERRORS

We have taken you through exercises that illustrate a number of ways in which reasoning may be faulty. We have not listed all the ways, but we have given you a good start. We have saved some additional fallacies for later chapters because you are most likely to spot them when you focus on the particular question central to that chapter. As you encounter each additional fallacy, be sure to add it to your fallacy list.

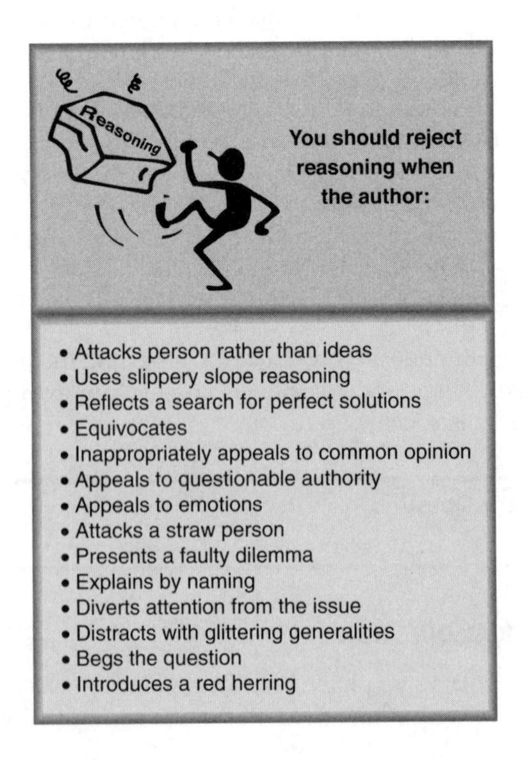

To find reasoning fallacies, keep in mind what kinds of reasons are good reasons—that is, the evidence and the moral principles relevant to the issue. Reasoning should be *rejected* whenever you have found mistaken assumptions, distractions, or support for the conclusion that already assumes the truth of the conclusion. Reasoning should be *approached cautiously* when it appeals to group-approved attitudes and to authority. You should always ask, "Are there good reasons to consider such appeals as persuasive evidence?" A precautionary note is in order here: Do not automatically reject reasoning that relies on appeals to authority or group-approved attitudes. Carefully evaluate such reasoning. For example, if most physicians in the country choose to take up jogging, that information is important to consider in deciding whether jogging is beneficial. Some authorities do possess valuable information. Because of their importance as a source of evidence, we discuss appeals to authority in detail in Chapter 7.

EXPANDING YOUR KNOWLEDGE OF FALLACIES

We recommend that you consult texts and some Web sites to expand your awareness and understanding of reasoning fallacies. Damer's *Attacking Faulty Reasoning* is an especially good source to help you become more familiar with reasoning fallacies.

Online Help: See suggestions for further engagement with fallacies at http://www.pearsonhighered.com/browne.

FALLACIES AND YOUR OWN WRITING AND SPEAKING

When you communicate, you necessarily engage in reasoning. If your purpose is to present a well-reasoned argument, in which you do not want to trick the reader into agreeing with you, then you will want to avoid committing reasoning fallacies. Awareness of possible errors committed by writers provides you with warnings to heed when you construct your own arguments. You can avoid fallacies by checking your own assumptions very carefully, by remembering that most controversial issues require you to get specific about advantages and disadvantages, and by keeping a checklist handy of possible reasoning fallacies.

PRACTICE EXERCISES

Critical Question: ***Are there any fallacies in the reasoning?***

Try to identify fallacies in the reasoning in each of the three practice passages.

Passage 1

The surgeon general has overstepped his bounds by recommending that explicit sex education begin as early as third grade. It is obvious that he is yet another victim of the AIDS hysteria sweeping the nation. Unfortunately, his media-influenced announcement has given new life to those who favor explicit sex education—even to the detriment of the nation's children.

Sexuality has always been a topic of conversation reserved for the family. Sex education has recently been forced on young children. The surgeon general's recommendation removes the role of the family entirely. It should be up to parents to explain sex to their children in a manner with which they are comfortable. Sex education exclusive of the family is stripped of values or any sense of morality, and should be discouraged. For years, families have taken the responsibility of sex education, and that's the way it should remain.

Passage 2

Pit bulls are unfairly discriminated against by the public because of hysterical overreactions to a few cases of the dogs acting violently. Only an idiot would ban this dog breed. Most of the complaints about pit bulls come from dog haters, people who tend to be frightened of dogs. I've had my loyal and loving pit bull Andy for over seven years and he has always been well behaved. I am confident that he could never attack a human being. Also, Dr. Overt, director of a local dog clinic has stated that most pit bulls are not unusually aggressive. Clearly placing some kind of ban on pits bulls would be a futile gesture. I have seen other dogs, such as golden retrievers, attack people. Thus, banning pit bulls would not totally prevent dog attacks on humans. And once outlawing pit bulls is permissible, the next step will be to ban any dog that has the potential for violence.

Passage 3

Bill: Countries that harbor terrorists who want to destroy the United States must be considered enemies of the United States. Any country that does not relinquish terrorists to the American justice system is clearly on the side of the terrorists. This sort of action means that the leaders of these countries do not wish to see justice done to the terrorists and care more about hiding murderers, rapists, thieves, and anti-democrats.

Taylor: That's exactly the kind of argument that I would expect from someone who has relatives who have worked for the CIA. But it seems to me that once you start labeling countries that disagree with America on policy as enemies, then eventually almost all countries will be considered our enemies, and we will be left with no allies.

Sample Responses

Passage 1

CONCLUSION: *Sex education should not be taught in schools.*

REASONS:
1. *The surgeon general's report reflects hysteria.*
2. *The surgeon general has been influenced by AIDS hysteria and the media.*
3. *The report removes the role of the family entirely.*
4. *Sex education is the job of parents; that's the way it has been and that's the way it should be.*

The author begins the argument by attacking the surgeon general rather than the issue. She claims that the recommendation is a by-product of the AIDS hysteria rather than extensive research. Her suggestion that the surgeon general issues reports in reaction to hot topics in the media undermines his credibility and character and is therefore *ad hominem.*

The second reason is a *straw-person fallacy* because it implies that the goal of sex education is to supply *all* the child's sex education.

Her third reason confuses "what is" with "what should be," and thus is an example of *wishful thinking.* Because sex education *should be* up to the parents does not mean that they *will* provide education.

The fourth reason presents a false dilemma—either keep sex education out of the schools or face morally loose, value-free children. But isn't it possible to have morally loose children even when sex education is taking place in the home? Isn't it also a possibility that both parents and the schools can play a role in sex education? Might not education result in children who are prepared to handle the issue of sex in their lives better than morally deficient delinquents?

Passage 2

CONCLUSION: *Pit bulls should not be banned.*

REASONS:
1. *Desire to ban results from hysterical public reaction to just a few cases.*
2. *Most complaints come from dog haters.*
3. *Owner knows pit bull would never attack anyone.*
4. *Banning pit bulls wouldn't solve the problem; there would still be attacks by other breeds.*
5. *Dog clinic director states that most pit bulls are not unusually aggressive.*
6. *Banning pit bulls would lead to banning other breeds.*

This essay begins with *ad hominem* and *name-calling* fallacies, attacking the character of those who want to ban pit bull dogs rather than addressing any specific arguments. *Wishful thinking* appears to influence the writer's third reason, and the fourth reason commits the fallacy of *search for a perfect solution*. Reducing the number of violent dog attacks would solve some of the problem, even if not all the problem of violent dog attacks. His next reason illustrates the *slippery slope fallacy*, as it is clearly possible to make laws that ban one breed of dog without extending such laws to other breeds. In his last reason, the author commits the *ad populum fallacy* by mistakenly assuming that because many people have such a belief about dogs, that belief is true.

CHAPTER

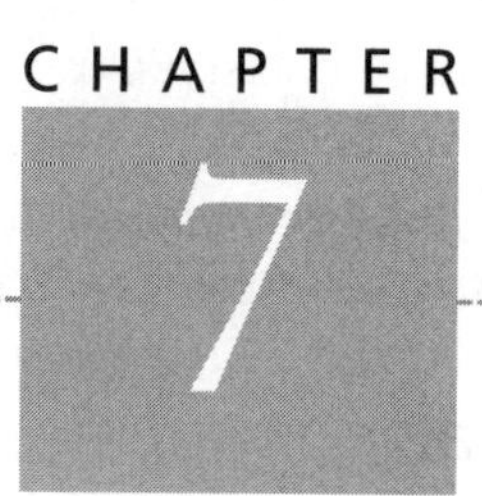

How Good Is the Evidence: Intuition, Personal Experience, Case Examples, Testimonials, and Appeals to Authority?

In the last chapter, you made major inroads into the process of evaluating persuasive communications by learning how to detect some fallacies in reasoning. In the following chapters, we continue our focus on evaluation as we learn to ask critical questions about a specific part of the reasoning structure: claims about the "facts." Let's see what such claims look like.

> Practicing yoga reduces the risk of cancer.
>
> Playing video games increases hand–eye coordination.
>
> More college students are coming to classes with hangovers. *Time* magazine reports that 24 percent of college students report attending a class at least once in the last two weeks while experiencing a hangover from drinking too much the night before.

What do we make of these claims? Are they legitimate? Most reasoning includes claims such as these. In this chapter, we begin the process of evaluating such claims.

Critical Question: ***How good is the evidence: intuition, personal experience, case examples, testimonials, and appeals to authority?***

THE NEED FOR EVIDENCE

Almost all reasoning we encounter includes beliefs about the way the world was, is, or is going to be that the communicator wants us to accept as "facts." These beliefs can be conclusions, reasons, or assumptions. We can refer to such beliefs as *factual claims.*

The first question you should ask about a factual claim is, "*Why should I believe it?*"

Your next question is, "*Does the claim need evidence to support it?*" If it does, and if there is no evidence, the claim is a *mere assertion, meaning a claim that is not backed up in any way.* You should seriously question the dependability of mere assertions!

If there is evidence, your next question is, "*How good is the evidence?*"

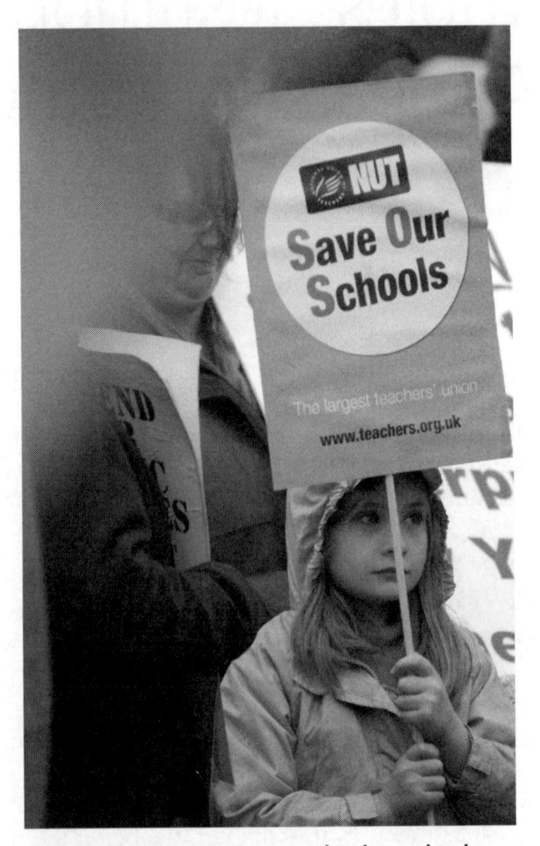

What evidence suggests our schools need to be saved? © Getty Images

To evaluate reasoning, we need to remember that some factual claims can be counted on more than others. For example, you probably feel quite certain that the claim "most U.S. senators are men" is true, but less certain that the assertion "practicing yoga reduces the risk of cancer" is true.

Because it is extremely difficult, if not impossible, to establish the *absolute* truth or falsity of most claims, rather than asking whether they are *true*, we prefer to ask whether they are *dependable*. In essence, we want to ask, "*Can we count on such beliefs?*" The greater the quality and quantity of evidence supporting a claim, the more we can *depend on it*, and the more we can call the claim a "*fact*."

For example, abundant evidence exists that George Washington was the first president of the United States of America. Thus, we can treat that claim as a fact. On the other hand, there is much conflicting evidence for the belief "bottled water is safer to drink than tap water." We thus can't treat this belief as a fact. The major difference between claims that are *opinions* and those that are *facts* is the present state of the relevant evidence. The more supporting evidence there is for a belief, the more "factual" the belief becomes.

Before we judge the persuasiveness of a communication, we need to know which factual claims are most dependable. How do we determine dependability? We ask questions like the following:

What is your proof?	How do you know that's true?
Where's the evidence?	Why do you believe that?
Are you sure that's true?	Can you prove it?

You will be well on your way to being among the best critical thinkers when you develop the habit of regularly asking these questions. They require those making arguments to be responsible by revealing the basis for their arguments. Anyone with an argument that you should consider will not hesitate to answer these questions. They know they have substantial support for their claims and, consequently, will want to share their evidence in the hope that you will learn to share their conclusions. When people react to simple requests for evidence with anger or withdrawal, they usually do so because they are embarrassed as they realize that, without evidence, they should have been less assertive about their beliefs.

When we regularly ask these questions, we notice that for many beliefs there is insufficient evidence to clearly support or refute them. For example, much evidence supports the assertion that taking an aspirin every other day reduces the risk of heart attack, although some other evidence disputes it. In such cases, we need to make judgments about where the *preponderance of evidence* lies as we decide on the dependability of the factual claim.

Making such judgments requires us to ask the important question, "*How good is the evidence?*" Chapters 7 to 9 focus on questions we need to ask to decide how well communicators have supported their factual claims. The more dependable the factual claims, the more persuasive the communications.

LOCATING FACTUAL CLAIMS

We encounter factual claims as (a) *descriptive conclusions*, (b) *reasons* used to support either descriptive or prescriptive conclusions, or (c) *descriptive assumptions*. Let's examine an example of each within brief arguments.

(a) Frequent use of headphones may cause hearing loss. Researchers studied the frequency and duration of headphone use among 251 college students and found that 49 percent of the students showed evidence of hearing impairment.

Note that *"frequent use of headphones may cause hearing loss"* is a factual claim that is a descriptive conclusion supported by research evidence. In this case, we want to ask, "Is that conclusion—a factual claim—justified by the evidence?"

(b) This country needs tougher gun regulations. The number of gun-related crimes has increased over the last 10 years.

Note that the factual claim here is that *"the number of gun-related crimes has increased over the last 10 years,"* and it functions as a reason supporting a prescriptive conclusion. In this case, we want to ask, "Is that reason—a factual claim—justified by the evidence?"

(c) Professors need to include more active discussions in their classrooms because too many college graduates lack critical thinking skills.

An unstated descriptive assumption links the reason to the conclusion: *Students learn how to think critically by participating in active classroom discussions.*

This factual claim is a descriptive assumption, which may or may not be dependable. Before we believe the assumption, and thus the reason, we want to ask, "How well does evidence support the assumption?" You will find that while many communicators perceive the desirability of supporting their reasons with evidence, they don't see the need to make their assumptions explicit. Thus, evidence for assumptions is rarely presented, even though in many cases such evidence would be quite helpful in deciding the quality of an argument.

SOURCES OF EVIDENCE

When should we accept a factual claim as dependable? There are three instances in which we will be most inclined to agree with a factual claim:

1. when the claim appears to be undisputed common knowledge, such as the claim "weight lifting increases muscular body mass";
2. when the claim is the conclusion from a well-reasoned argument; and

3. when the claim is adequately supported by solid evidence in the same communication or by other evidence that we know.

Our concern in this chapter is the third instance. Determining the adequacy of evidence requires us to ask, *"How good is the evidence?"* To answer this question, we must first ask, "What do we mean by *evidence?*"

Attention: *Evidence is explicit information shared by the communicator that is used to back up or to justify the dependability of a factual claim (see Chapter 2). In prescriptive arguments, evidence will be needed to support reasons that are factual claims; in descriptive arguments, evidence will be needed to directly support a descriptive conclusion.*

The quality of evidence depends on the kind of evidence it is. Thus, to evaluate evidence, we first need to ask, *"What kind of evidence is it?"* Knowing the kind of evidence tells us what questions we should ask.

When used appropriately, each kind of evidence can be "good evidence." It can help support an author's claim. Like a gold prospector closely examining the gravel in her pan for potentially high-quality ore, we must closely examine the evidence to determine its quality. We want to know, "Does an author's evidence provide dependable support for her claim?" Thus, we begin to evaluate evidence by asking, *"How good is the evidence?"* Always keep in the back of your mind that no evidence will be a slam dunk that gets the job done conclusively. You are looking for better evidence; searching for altogether wonderful evidence will be frustrating.

In this chapter and in Chapter 8, we examine the kinds of questions we can ask of each type of evidence to help us decide its quality. Kinds of

EXHIBIT 7-1 Major Kinds of Evidence

✓ intuition
✓ personal experiences
✓ case examples
✓ testimonials
✓ appeals to authorities or experts
✓ personal observations
✓ research studies
✓ analogies

evidence examined in this chapter are intuition, personal experiences, case examples, testimonials, and appeals to authority.

INTUITION AS EVIDENCE

> "I just sense that Janette is the right girl for me, even though my friends think we're a bad match."
>
> "I just have this feeling that Senator Ramirez will surprise the pollsters and win the election."
>
> "I can tell immediately that this slot machine is going to be a winner for me today."

When we use intuition to support a claim, we rely on "common sense," or on our "gut feelings," or on hunches. Listen to Jewell celebrating intuition as a source of understanding:

> *Follow your heart*
> *Your intuition*
> *It will lead you in the right direction*
> *Let go of your mind*
> *Your Intuition*
> *It's easy to find*
> *—Jewel, "Intuition"*

When a communicator supports a claim by saying "common sense tells us" or "I just know that it's true," she is using intuition as her evidence. Intuition refers to a process in which we believe we have direct insights about something without being able to consciously express our reasons.

A major problem with intuition is that it is private; others have no way to judge its dependability. Thus, when intuitive beliefs differ, as they so often do, we have no solid basis for deciding which ones to believe. Also, much intuition relies on unconscious processing that largely ignores relevant evidence and reflects strong biases. Consequently, we must be very wary of claims backed up only by intuition.

However, sometimes "intuition" may in fact be relying on some other kind of evidence, such as extensive relevant personal experiences and readings, that have been unconsciously accessed from somewhere in our mind. For example, when an experienced pilot has an intuition that the plane doesn't feel right as it taxis for takeoff, we might be quite supportive of further safety checks of the plane prior to takeoff. Sometimes, hunches are not blind, just incapable of explanation. As critical thinkers, we would want to find out whether claims relying on intuition have any other kinds of evidential support.

PERSONAL EXPERIENCE AS EVIDENCE

The following arguments use a particular kind of evidence to support a factual claim.

> "My friend Judy does really well on her tests when she stays up all night to study for them; so I don't see the need for getting sleep before taking tomorrow's test."
>
> "I always feel better after having a big slice of chocolate cake, so I think that anyone who is depressed just needs to eat more chocolate cake."

Both arguments appeal to personal experiences as evidence. Phrases like "I know someone who . . .," and "In my experience, I've found . . ." should alert you to such evidence. Because personal experiences are very vivid in our memories, we often rely on them as evidence to support a belief. For example, you might have a really frustrating experience with a car mechanic because she greatly overcharges you for her services, leading you to believe that most car mechanics overcharge. While the generalization about car mechanics may or may not be true, relying on such experiences as the basis for a general belief is a mistake! Because a single personal experience, or even an accumulation of personal experiences, is not enough to give you a *representative* sample of experiences, personal experiences often lead us to commit the *hasty generalization* fallacy. A single striking experience or several such experiences can demonstrate that certain outcomes are *possible*; for example, you may have met several people who claim their lives were saved because they were not wearing their seat belts when they got into a car accident. Such experiences, however, cannot demonstrate that such outcomes are *typical* or *probable*. Be wary when you hear yourself or others arguing, "Well, in my experience. . . ."

Fallacy: Hasty Generalization: A person draws a conclusion about a large group based on experiences with only a few members of the group.

We will revisit this fallacy in Chapter 8 when we discuss research evidence and issues of sampling.

CASE EXAMPLES AS EVIDENCE

> President of a large university: "Of course our students can move on to high paying jobs and further study at large universities. Why, just this past year we sent one of our students, Mary Nicexample, off to law school at Harvard. In her first year, Mary remained in the top 5 percent of her class. Therefore, our students can certainly achieve remarkable success at elite universities."

A frequently used kind of evidence is the use of a detailed catchy description of, or story about, one or several individuals or events to support a conclusion. Such descriptions are usually based on observations or interviews and vary from being in-depth to being superficial. We call such descriptions *case examples*. Communicators often begin persuasive presentations with dramatic descriptions of some event to emotionally involve their audience. For example, one way to argue for the banning of cell phone use in cars is to tell heart-wrenching stories of young people dying in car accidents because the driver was talking on a cell phone.

Case examples are often compelling to us because of their colorfulness and their interesting details, which make them easy to visualize. Political candidates have increasingly resorted to case examples in their speeches, knowing that the rich details of cases generate an emotional reaction.

Because dramatic cases *appeal to our emotions*, they distract us from paying close attention to their value as evidence and from seeking other more relevant research evidence. For example, imagine a story about a man who tortured and murdered his numerous victims. The emotions triggered by such a story are likely to increase our desire for capital punishment. Yet, the human drama of these crimes may lead us to ignore the fact that such a case is rare and that over the past 30 years, 119 inmates with capital sentences were found to be innocent and released from prison.

Be wary of striking case examples as proof!

Although case examples will be consistent with a conclusion, do not let that consistency fool you. Always ask yourself: "Is the example typical?" "Are there powerful counterexamples?" "Are there biases in how the example is reported?"

Are there times that case examples can be useful, even if they are not good evidence? Certainly! Like personal experiences, they demonstrate important *possibilities* and put a personal face on abstract statistics. They make it easier for people to relate to an issue and thus take more interest in it.

TESTIMONIALS AS EVIDENCE

> Note on service station wall: "Jane did a wonderful job fixing the oil leak my car had. I strongly recommend that you take your car to Jane to fix any engine problem you have."
>
> This book looks great. On the back cover, comments from readers say, "I could not put this book down."

Commercials, ads for movies, recommendations on the backs of book jackets, and "proofs" of the existence of the paranormal or other controversial or extraordinary life events often try to persuade by using a special kind of appeal to personal experience; they quote particular persons, often a celebrity, as saying that a given idea or product is good or bad, or that extraordinary events have occurred, based upon their personal experiences. Such quoted statements serve as *personal testimonials*. You may have listened to personal testimonials from college students when you chose your college. Testimonials are thus a form of personal experience in which someone (often a celebrity) provides a statement supporting the value of some product, event, or service and the endorsement lacks any of the information we would need to decide just how much we should let it influence us.

How helpful is such evidence? Usually, it is not very helpful at all. In most cases, we should pay little attention to personal testimonials until we find out much more about the expertise, interests, values, and biases behind them. We should be especially wary of each of the following problems with testimonials:

- **Selectivity.** People's experiences differ greatly. Those trying to persuade us have usually carefully selected the testimony they use. What we are most likely to see on the back of a book jacket is the BEST PRAISE, not the most typical reaction. We should always ask the question, "What was the experience like for those whom we have not heard from?" Also, people who provide the testimonials have often been selective in their attention, paying special attention to information that confirms their beliefs and ignoring disconfirming information. Often, believing is seeing! Our *expectancies* greatly influence how we experience events. If we believe that aliens live among us, or that humans never really landed on the moon, then we are more likely to see ambiguous images as aliens or as proof of the government conspiracy regarding the moon landing.
- **Personal interest.** Many testimonials such as those used for books, movies, and television products come from people who have something to gain from their testimony. For example, drug companies often give doctors grants to do research, as long as they prescribe the drug company's brands of medication. Thus, we need to ask, "Does the person providing the testimony have a relationship with what he is advocating such that we can expect a strong bias in his testimony?"
- **Omitted information.** Testimonials rarely provide sufficient information about the basis for the judgment. For example, when a friend of yours encourages you to go see this new movie because it is the "best movie ever," you should ask, with warmth, about what makes the movie so impressive. Our standards for judgment may well differ from the standards of those giving the testimony.
- **The human factor.** One reason that testimonials are so convincing is that they come from very enthusiastic people, who seem trustworthy, well-meaning, and honest. Such people make us *want* to believe them.

APPEALS TO AUTHORITY AS EVIDENCE

> According to my doctor, I should be taking antidepressant drugs to help me cope with my recent episodes of depression and I don't need to worry about side effects.

The speaker has defended his claim by appealing to authority—sources that are supposed to know more than most of us about a given topic—so-called experts. When communicators appeal to authorities or experts, they appeal to people who they believe are in a position to have access to certain facts and to have special qualifications for drawing conclusions from the facts. Thus, such appeals potentially provide more oomph to an argument than testimonials, depending on the background of the authority. You encounter appeals to many forms of authority on a daily basis. And you have little choice but to rely on them because you have neither the time nor the knowledge to become adept in more than a few dimensions of our very complicated lives.

Movie reviewers: "One of the ten best movies of the year." Valerie Viewer, Toledo Gazette.

Talk show pundits: "The economy is heading for a recession."

Organizations: "The American Medical Association supports this position."

Researchers: "Studies show . . ."

Relatives: "My grandfather says . . ."

Religion: "The Koran says . . ."

Magazines: "According to Newsweek . . ."

We can get expert advice from such sources on how to lose weight, achieve happiness, get rich, lower cholesterol, raise a well-adjusted child, and catch a big fish. You can easily add to our list.

It should be obvious that some appeals to authority should be taken much more seriously as evidence than others. Why? Some authorities are much more careful in giving an opinion than others. For example, *Newsweek* and *Time* are much more likely to carefully evaluate the available evidence prior to stating an opinion than is the *National Enquirer*. Articles on schizophrenia are more likely to be based on carefully collected evidence if they are posted on the National Institute of Mental Health Web site than if they are posted on a personal Web page. Our relatives are much less likely than editorial writers for major newspapers to have systematically evaluated a political candidate.

You should remember that *authorities are often wrong*. Also, they often disagree. The following examples, taken from *The Experts Speak*, are clear reminders of the fallibility of expert opinion (Christopher Cerf and Victor Navasky, 1998, Rev. Ed., Villard Books, New York).

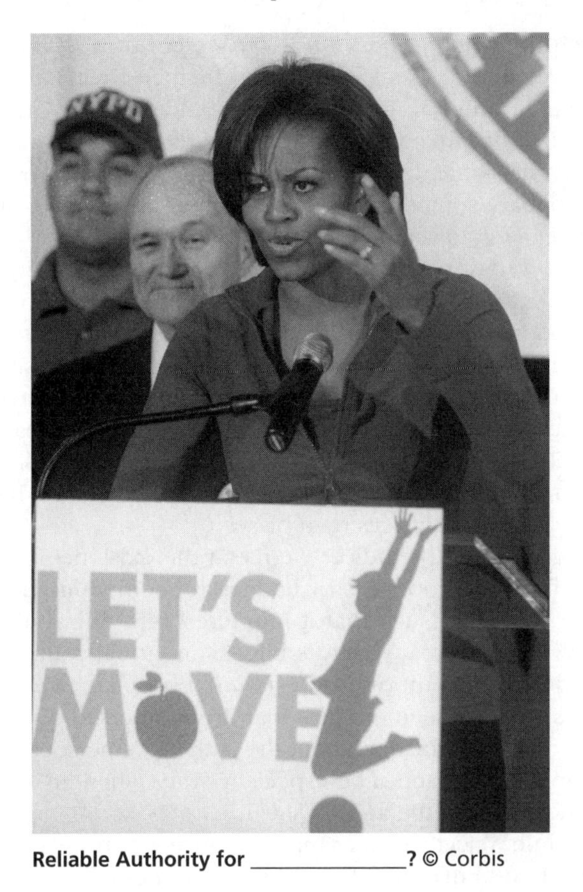

Reliable Authority for _____________? © Corbis

"I think there is a world market for maybe five computers."
—Thomas Watson, chairman of IBM, 1943.

"Video won't be able to hold onto any market it captures after the first six months. People will soon get tired of staring at a plywood box every night."
—Darryl F. Zanuck, Head of Twentieth Century Fox Studios, ca. 1946.

These quotes should remind us that we need to ask critical questions when communicators appeal to authority. We need to ask, "*Why should we believe this authority?*" More specifically, we should ask the following questions of authorities.

How much expertise, training, or special knowledge does the authority have about the subject about which he is communicating? Is this a topic the person has studied for a long time? Or, has the person had extensive experience related to the topic?

Was the authority in a position to have especially good access to pertinent facts? For example, was she involved firsthand with the events about which she makes claims? In general, you should be more impressed by an authority who is a *primary source*—someone having firsthand involvement with relevant events—than by *secondary sources. Time* and *Newsweek*, for example, are secondary sources, while research journals such as the *Journal of the American Medical Association* are primary sources.

Is there good reason to believe that the authority is relatively free of distorting influences? Among the factors that can influence how evidence is reported are personal needs, prior expectations, general beliefs, attitudes, values, theories, and ideologies. For example, if a public university president is asked whether cuts in funding for education are bad for the university, he will in all probability answer "yes" and give a number of good reasons. He may be giving an unbiased view of the situation. Because of his position, however, we would want to be concerned about the possibility that he has sought out only those reasons that justify his own biases.

By having bias and prejudice, we mean the existence of a strong personal feeling about the goodness or badness of something up front before we look at the evidence, such that it interferes with our ability to evaluate evidence fairly. Because many factors bias us in virtually all our judgments, we cannot expect any authority to be *totally* unbiased. We can, however, expect less bias from some authorities than from others and try to determine such bias by seeking information about the authority's personal interest in the topic. For example, we want to be especially wary when an authority stands to benefit financially from the actions she advocates.

We should not reject a claim simply because we suspect that the authority's personal interests may interfere with her fairness. One helpful step we can take is to check to see whether authorities with diverse attitudes, prior expectations, values, and interests agree. Thus, it is also helpful to ask the questions: "*Has the authority developed a reputation for frequently making dependable claims?*"

You will want to be especially concerned about the quality of authorities when you encounter factual claims on the Internet. When we go online, virtually everyone becomes a potential "authority" because people are free to claim whatever they wish, and there is no built-in process to evaluate such claims. It is clearly a "buyers beware" situation!

You should strive to learn as much as you can about the purpose of Web sites, the credentials and experience of the contributors associated with them, and the nature of the reasoning support provided for their conclusions. Pay very close attention to the reasoning structure. Check to see whether the site is associated with or linked to highly reputable sites.

Further clues that the site may be undependable include a lack of dates associated with postings, an unprofessional look to the site, claims that are vague, sweeping (e.g., "always," "never"), and emotional, rather than carefully qualified, a totally one-sided view, the absence of primary source evidence, the presence of hearsay evidence, and numerous reasoning fallacies. Finally, seek out evidence on the same topic from other sites.

Problems with Citers Citing Other Citers

A particularly troublesome kind of appeal to authority that has become increasingly frequent as the sizes of many news staffs have dwindled is a situation in which one authority supports an opinion by citing another authority. For example, one paper (e.g., the *New York Times*) cites another paper (e.g., the *Washington Post*), or one news service (e.g., Reuters) cites another news service (e.g., the Associated Press). Such citations give an illusion of supportive evidence but bypass the most basic question: How dependable was the original authority's claim to begin with? Citings of other citers are as informative as reading the same newspaper article over and over again hoping to learn something new. A related problem is the citing of "unnamed sources," or the reference to "some say . . ." Be especially cautious when you encounter appeals to authority that make it very difficult to pin down the basis for the original claims.

USING THIS CRITICAL QUESTION

When you identify problems with intuition, personal experience, case examples, testimonials, and appeals to authority as evidence, you have a proper basis for hesitating to accept the conclusion based on that evidence. Knowing these problems gives you some protection against bogus reasoning. However, you do want to work hard to be fair to the arguments that people present for your consideration. So it makes sense to ask those who provide you with insubstantial evidence whether they can give you some better evidence. Give arguments every chance they deserve.

EVIDENCE AND YOUR WRITING AND SPEAKING

As a writer, you should expect that your readers are also interested in arguments that are supported by strong evidence. Your readers may accept or reject your argument on the basis of your evidence. You should incorporate evidence into your writing as though your readers have your training and expectations. Let's consider this suggestion further.

Anticipating Critical Readers

How can you be prepared for readers who have the same set of questions in their toolbox and the same expectations about evidence as you do? You step into their shoes. You anticipate the critical questions that you would ask about the evidence if you were the reader. Then try to answer those questions preemptively. Tell your readers as much as you can about the evidence you have provided. Who published it? Do the authors or the institution who funded the research have any clear biases? What is their background? How current are the data? How generalizable is an observation or experience? Did you notice any potential problems with the evidence such as limited sample size or omitted information?

After you bring these concerns to the surface, you will be faced with a judgment call. You must decide whether you have provided enough evidence of strong quality. The decision is not an easy one—every piece of evidence comes with strengths and weaknesses. While we cannot give you a clear-cut set of rules to identify whether your argument needs more evidence or better evidence, we do have a couple rules of thumb.

Determining Whether You Need More Evidence

The more controversial your conclusion or your reason, the more time you should dedicate to providing evidence. Your audience should quickly accept information that is relatively indisputable, for instance, the name of the governor of Massachusetts, the number of years the sitcom *Friends* aired, or the capital of Qatar. Your audience will be less willing to accept a controversial point, such as Deval Patrick should be reelected to the governorship, *Friends* influenced style in the late 1990s more than any other sitcom, or Qatar should host the FIFA World Cup in 2022. These claims are disputable, and, as such, your readers will expect much more from you in terms of evidence before they accept your conclusion.

Lastly, you should pay particular attention to arguments that rely on one testimonial, an appeal to authority, or other types of evidence less regarded in academic writing. These sections may warrant more evidence. Our next section will indicate why.

Your Academic Writing and Evidence

When you commit to a writing project, you also commit to adhere to a set of writing conventions and expectations. Many of these conventions and expectations relate to writing style, for instance, the decision whether to avoid contractions or obscenities. These conventions change based on the circumstances—it may be appropriate to insert an impassioned explicative on a Web forum with friends, but inappropriate to do so in a formal report to your supervisor. This guideline extends to the types of evidence you choose to include in your writing. Some of the evidence we outlined in this chapter tends to be more appropriate for casual writing and communicating, such as writing a review of a new restaurant on Urbanspoon.com or urging your fellow gamers to download the new expansion pack for your multiplayer online role-playing game. We suspect, however, that much of your writing over the next few years of your life will be academic writing. Academic writing comes with certain expectations about the quality of the evidence. Expectations vary depending on the discipline, but they share certain similarities. When you understand these expectations, they can guide you as you make decisions about whether to bulk up your argument with more evidence.

In academic writing, a high value is placed on research that is publicly verifiable, conducted according to the scientific method, and reviewed by the authors' peers before publication. These standards improve the reliability of evidence. They make observations more generalizable. We will discuss why in Chapter 8. For now, keep an eye out in your academic writing for reasons supported by intuition, personal experience, testimonials or appeals to authority. You will probably want to back up these sections with peer-reviewed studies, polls with vigorous research methods, and research conducted with academic standards in mind. In academic writing, your audience will expect and appreciate this evidence.

In this chapter, we have focused on the evaluation of several kinds of evidence used to support factual claims: intuition, personal experience and anecdotes, testimonials, and appeals to authorities. Such evidence must be relied on with caution. We have provided you with some questions you should ask to determine whether such evidence is *good evidence*. In Chapter 8, we discuss other kinds of evidence, as we continue to ask the question, "*How good is the evidence?*"

PRACTICE EXERCISES

Critical Question: ***How good is the evidence: intuition, personal experience, case examples, testimonials, and appeals to authority?***

Evaluate the evidence in the following three passages.

Passage 1

Some well-known basketball players trying to get an edge on the competition have found a cheap and powerful device to improve their shooting ability, the HeadsUp Headband. According to the company that makes them, the band is made of material that interacts with the head's natural energy field in such a way that shooting concentration is greatly enhanced. Star players now wearing the headband commented about them during interviews with an ESPN sports writer:

Lenny Bigscorer: "I wouldn't play without one now. I can actually feel each shot heading for the sweet spot of the basket."

Dunkin Daniels: "It's amazing. I've never had my head so into the game of basketball. I'm encouraging the entire team to use them."

Passage 2

Are Botox injections a safe alternative to face-lifts? According to an interview with Dr. N.O. Worries published in *Cosmo*, there are no dangerous side effects associated with Botox injections. Dr. Worries performs hundreds of Botox injections each month, is well established as a physician in New York City, and has her own private practice. She claims she has never had a serious problem with any of her injections, and her patients have never reported any side effects. Furthermore, Hollywood's Association for Cosmetic Surgeons officially stated in a press release that Botox has never been shown to cause any negative effects, despite what other physicians might argue.

Passage 3

Are Macs really better than PCs? The answer is a resounding yes! *Computer Nerds Quarterly* recently ran an article thoroughly outlining every advantage that Macs have over PCs. Furthermore, just ask Mac users and they will quickly explain how Macs are superior to PCs. For example, Sherry, a Mac user, states, "My Mac is the best thing I ever purchased. It is fast and easy to use. Plus, it has never crashed on me. All of my friends who have PCs have complained about all kinds of problems my Mac has never had." More importantly, a recent report in *Consumer Affairs* states that more new businesses are using Mac-based systems than PC-based systems. Clearly, Macs are a cut above the PCs.

Sample Responses

Passage 1

CONCLUSION: *Wearing HeadsUp Headbands is boosting performance in star basketball players.*

REASON: *Famous basketball players rave about the positive impact of the headbands.*

We should not rely on these testimonials as good "proof." This passage illustrates well the weaknesses of testimony as evidence as well as the power of expectations in affecting perceptions. How typical are these success stories? Would randomly selected users of the headband have voiced so much praise? Have the players actually improved their shooting; if so, is the improvement just a chance event? Are there other causes for the improvement? Are these selected athletes highly suggestible? Until more systematic research data are collected, we should not conclude that these headbands cause improved shooting performance in basketball players.

Passage 2

CONCLUSION: *Botox injections are safe.*

REASON: *A cosmetic surgeon and a state professional organization claim Botox is safe.*

How much should we depend on these appeals to authority? Not much. First, both authorities are likely to be very biased. They stand to gain financially by making safety claims. Dr. Worries's testimony is especially suspect because it is based on her experiences only. She has probably not sought out evidence of failures. The claims of the professional organization are as questionable as those of Dr. Worries because the organization is comprised of cosmetic surgeons, who probably perform Botox injections. If the organization were to have offered some sort of systematic research for why Botox is safe, perhaps its claims would be less suspect.

CHAPTER

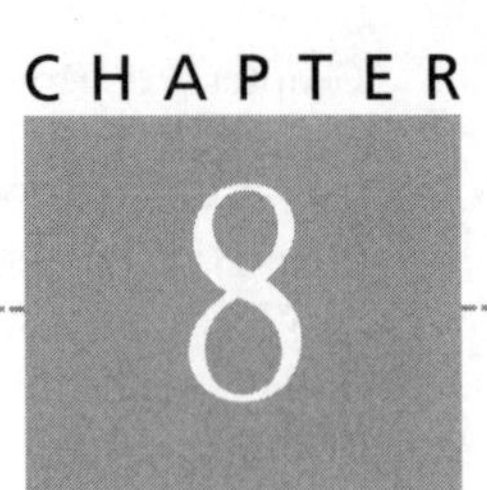

How Good Is the Evidence: Personal Observation, Research Studies, and Analogies?

In this chapter, we continue our evaluation of evidence. We focus on three common kinds of evidence: personal observation, research studies, and analogies. We need to question each of these when we encounter them as evidence.

Critical Question: ***How good is the evidence: personal observation, research studies, and analogies?***

PERSONAL OBSERVATION AS EVIDENCE

> The policeman who shot and killed an unarmed man should be charged with a crime. Although he claims he thought the victim was reaching for a gun, onlookers reported that the victim was not making a threatening movement.

How much can we count on the observation of such onlookers? One valuable kind of evidence is personal observation, the basis for much everyday reasoning as well as scientific research. For example, we feel confident of something we actually see. Thus, we tend to rely on eyewitness testimony as evidence. For many reasons, however, personal observations turn out to be untrustworthy evidence.

Observers, unlike certain mirrors, do not give us "pure" observations. What we "see" and report are filtered through a set of values, biases, attitudes, and expectations. We tend to see or hear what we wish to see or hear, selecting and remembering those aspects of an experience that are most consistent with our prior experience and background. In addition, many situations present major impediments to seeing accurately, such as poor attention, rapid movement of events observed, and stressful environments. Imagine for example possible distortions in your observation if you were standing near a person waving a gun at a bank teller.

When reports of observations in newspapers, magazines, books, television, and the Internet, as well as in research studies are used as evidence, you need to determine whether there are good reasons to rely on such reports. The most reliable reports will be based on recent observations made by several people observing under optimal conditions who have no apparent, strong expectations or biases related to the event being observed.

RESEARCH STUDIES AS EVIDENCE

"Studies show . . ."

"Research investigators have found in a recent survey that . . ."

"A report in the New England Journal of Medicine indicates . . ."

One form of authority that frequently relies a great deal on observation and often carries special weight is the research study: usually a systematic collection of observations by people trained to do scientific research. How dependable are research findings? As is true for appeals to authority in general, we cannot know the answers until we ask lots of questions.

Society has turned to the scientific method as an important guide for determining the facts because the relationships among events in our world are very complex, and because humans are fallible in their observations and theories about these events. The scientific method attempts to avoid many of the built-in biases in our observations of the world and in our intuition and common sense.

What is special about the scientific method? Above all, it seeks information in the form of *publicly verifiable data*—that is, data obtained under conditions such that other qualified people can make similar observations and get the same results. Thus, for example, if one researcher reports that she was able to achieve cold fusion in the lab, the experiment would seem more credible if other researchers could obtain the same results.

A second major characteristic of scientific method is *control*—that is, the use of special procedures to reduce error in observations and in the interpretation of research findings. For example, if bias in observations may be a major problem, researchers might try to control this kind of error by using multiple observers to see how well they agree with one another. Physical scientists frequently maximize control by studying problems in the laboratory so that they can minimize extraneous factors. Unfortunately, control is usually more difficult in the social world than in the physical world; thus, it is very difficult to successfully apply the scientific method to many questions about complex human behavior.

Precision in language is a third major component of the scientific method. Concepts are often confusing, obscure, and ambiguous. Scientific method tries to be precise and consistent in its use of language.

While there is much more to science than we can discuss here, we want you to keep in mind that scientific research, when conducted well, is one of our best sources of evidence because it emphasizes *verifiability*, *control*, and *precision*.

Problems with Research Findings

Unfortunately, the fact that research has been applied to a problem does not necessarily mean that the research evidence is dependable evidence or that the interpretations of the meaning of the evidence are accurate. Like appeals to any source, appeals to research evidence must be approached with caution. Also, some questions, particularly those that focus on human behavior, can be answered only tentatively even with the best of evidence. Therefore, we have to ask a number of important questions about research studies before we decide how much to depend on their conclusions.

When communicators appeal to research as a source of evidence, you should remember the following:

1. Research varies greatly in *quality*. There is well-done research and there is poorly done research, and we should rely more on the former. Because the research process is so complex and is subject to so many external influences, even those well trained in research practices sometimes conduct research studies that have important deficiencies; publication in a scientific journal does not guarantee that a research study is not flawed in important ways.
2. Research findings often contradict one another. Thus, *single* research studies presented out of the context of the family of research studies that investigate the question often provide misleading conclusions. Research findings that most deserve our attention are those that have been replicated by more than one researcher or group of researchers. Many claims never get retested, and many of those that are retested fail to replicate the original results. For example, a recent study published in a prestigious medical journal found that 41 percent of retestings of very highly regarded research claims of successful medical interventions convincingly showed the original claims to be wrong or greatly exaggerated (see "Lies, Damned Lies, and Medical Science," November 2010, *Atlantic Magazine*). We need to always ask the question: "Have other researchers verified the findings?"

3. Research findings *do not prove* conclusions. At best, they *support* conclusions. Such findings do not speak for themselves! Researchers must always *interpret* the meaning of their findings, and all findings can be interpreted in more than one way (see Chapter 7). Hence, researchers' conclusions should not be treated as demonstrated "truths." When you encounter statements such as "research findings show . . .," you should retranslate them into "researchers interpret their research findings as showing . . ."
4. Like all of us, researchers have expectations, attitudes, values, and needs that bias the questions they ask, the way they conduct their research, and the way they interpret their research findings. For example, scientists often have an emotional investment in a particular hypothesis. When the American Sugar Institute is paying for your summer research grant, it will be very difficult for you to find that sugar consumption among teenagers is excessive. Like all fallible human beings, scientists may find it difficult to objectively treat data that conflict with their hypothesis. A major strength of scientific research is that it tries to make public its procedures and results so that others can judge the merit of the research and then try to replicate it. However, regardless of how objective a scientific report may seem, important subjective elements are always involved.
5. Speakers and writers often distort or simplify research conclusions. Major discrepancies may occur between the conclusion merited by the original research and the use of the evidence to support a communicator's beliefs. For example, researchers may carefully qualify their own conclusions in their original research report only to have the conclusions used by others without the qualifications.
6. Research "facts" change over time, especially claims about human behavior. For example, the following research "facts" have been reported by major scientific sources, yet have been refuted by recent research evidence:

   - Prozac, Zoloft, and Paxil are more effective than a placebo for most cases of depression.
   - Taking fish oil, exercising, and doing puzzles helps fend off Alzheimer's disease.
   - Measles vaccine causes autism.

7. Research varies in how artificial it is. Often, to achieve the goal of control, research loses some of its real-world quality. The more artificial the research, the more difficult it is to generalize from the research study to the world outside. The problem of research artificiality is especially evident in research studying complex social behavior. For example, social scientists will have people sit in a room with a computer to play games that involve testing people's reasoning processes. The researchers are trying to figure out why people make certain decisions when confronted with different scenarios. However, we should ask, "Is sitting at the computer

while thinking through hypothetical situations too artificial to tell us much about the way people make decisions when confronted with real dilemmas?"

8. The need for financial gain, status, security, and other factors can affect research outcomes. Researchers are human beings, not computers. Thus, it is extremely difficult for them to be totally objective. For example, researchers who want to find a certain outcome through their research may interpret their results in such a way to find the desired outcome. Pressures to obtain grants, tenure, or other personal rewards might ultimately affect the way in which researchers interpret their data. For example, research studies funded by a pharmaceutical company tend to have a much higher rate of positive findings for drug interventions using that company's drugs than does research studying the same drugs funded by sponsors not associated with that drug company, such as federal government funding agencies.

As you can see, despite the many positive qualities of research evidence, we need to avoid embracing research conclusions prematurely. However, you should not REJECT a scientifically based conclusion just because there is SOME doubt associated with it. Certainty is often an impossible goal, but all conclusions are not equally uncertain, and we should be willing to embrace some conclusions much more than others. Thus, when critically evaluating

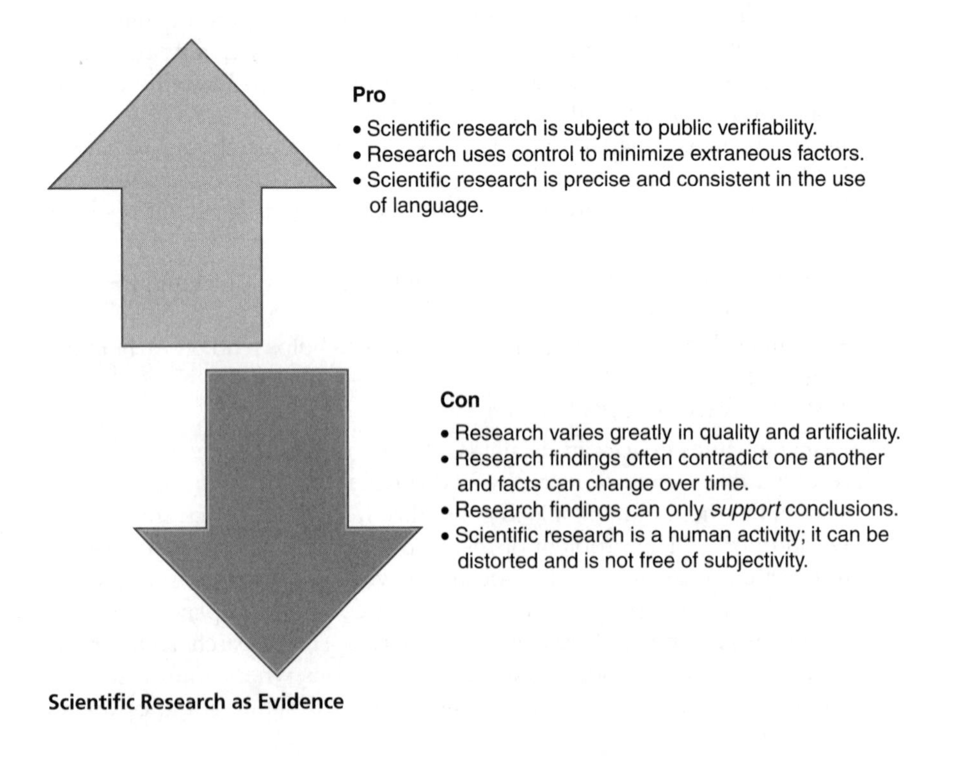

Scientific Research as Evidence

research conclusions, be wary of the reasoning error of demanding certainty in some conclusion when some uncertainty is to be expected but that does not negate the conclusion. We label this reasoning error the *impossible certainty fallacy*.

Fallacy: Impossible Certainty: Assuming that a research conclusion should be rejected if it is not absolutely certain.

Clues for Evaluating Research Studies

Apply the following questions to research findings to determine whether the findings are dependable evidence.

1. *What is the quality of the source of the report?* Usually, the most dependable reports are those published in peer-reviewed journals, those in which a study is not accepted until it has been reviewed by a series of relevant experts. Usually—but not always—the more reputable the source, the better designed the study. So, try to find out all you can about the reputation of the source.
2. Other than the quality of the source, are there other clues included in the communication suggesting the research was well done? For example, *does the report detail any special strengths of the research?* Unfortunately, most reports of research findings encountered in popular magazines, newspapers, television reports, and blogs fail to provide sufficient detail about the research to warrant our judgment of the research quality.
3. *How recently was the research conducted, and are there any reasons to believe that the findings might have changed over time?* Many research conclusions change over time. For example, the causes of depression, crime, or heart disease in 1980 may be quite different from those in 2010.
4. *Have the study's findings been replicated by other studies?* When an association is repeatedly and consistently found in well-designed studies—for example, the link between smoking and cancer—then there is reason to believe it, at least until those who disagree can provide persuasive evidence for their point of view.
5. *How selective has the communicator been in choosing studies?* For example, have relevant studies with contradictory results been omitted? Has the researcher selected only those studies that support his point?
6. *Is there any evidence of strong-sense critical thinking?* Has the speaker or writer showed a critical attitude toward earlier research that was supportive of her point of view? Most conclusions from research need to be qualified because of research limitations. Has the communicator demonstrated a willingness to qualify?
7. *Is there any reason for someone to have distorted the research?* We need to be wary of situations in which the researchers *need* to find certain kinds of results.

8. *Are conditions in the research artificial and therefore distorted?* Always ask, "How similar are the conditions under which the research study was conducted to the situation the researcher is generalizing about?"
9. *How far can we generalize, given the research sample?* Because this is such an important issue, we discuss it in depth in our next section.
10. *Are there any biases or distortions in the surveys, questionnaires, ratings, or other measurements that the researcher uses?* We need to have confidence that the researcher has measured accurately what she has wanted to measure. The problem of biased surveys and questionnaires is so pervasive in research that we discuss it in more detail in a later section.

GENERALIZING FROM THE RESEARCH SAMPLE

Speakers and writers usually use research reports to support generalizations, that is, claims about *events in general.* For example, "the medication was effective in treating cancer for 75 percent of the patients in the study" is not a generalization; "the medication cures pancreatic cancer" is. Most publicized generalizations that we encounter need to be closely examined for the possibility of overgeneralizing! Let's see why.

First, how we sample is crucial in determining to what extent we can generalize. The ability to generalize from research findings depends on the *number, breadth,* and *randomness* of events or people in the researcher's study. The process of selecting events or persons to study is called *sampling.*

Because researchers can never study all events or people about which they want to generalize, they must choose some way to sample; and some ways are preferable to others. You need to keep several important considerations in mind when evaluating the research sample:

1. The sample must be *large* enough to justify the generalization or conclusion. In most cases, the more events or people researchers observe, the more dependable their conclusion. If we want to form a general belief about how often college students receive help from others on term papers, we are better off studying 1,000 college students than studying 100.
2. The sample must possess as much *breadth*, or diversity, as the types of events about which conclusions are to be drawn. For example, if researchers want to generalize about college students' drinking habits in general, their evidence should be based on the sampling of a variety of different kinds of college students in a variety of different kinds of college settings.
3. The more *random* the sample, the better. When researchers randomly sample, they try to make sure that all events about which they want to generalize have an *equal chance* of getting sampled; they try to avoid a biased sample. Major polls, like the Gallup Poll, for example, always try to sample randomly. This keeps them from getting groups of events or

people that have biased characteristics. Do you see how each of the following samples has biased characteristics?

a. People who volunteer to be interviewed about frequency of sexual activity.
b. People who have land-line phones only.
c. Students in an introductory psychology class.
d. Viewers of particular television networks, such as Fox or MSNBC.

Thus, we want to ask of all research studies, "How many events or people did they sample, how much breadth did the sample have, and how random was the sample?"

Failure to attend sufficiently to the limits of sampling leads to *overgeneralizing* research findings, stating a generalization that is much broader than warranted by the research. In Chapter 7, we referred to such overgeneralization as the *hasty generalization fallacy*. Let's take a close look at a research overgeneralization:

> People who join online dating services tend to succeed in finding a good match. An online survey of 229 people, aged 18 to 65, who have used Internet dating sites, asked them about their main relationship that they had had online. The research showed that: 94 percent of those surveyed saw their 'e-partners' again after first meeting them, and the relationships lasted for an average of at least seven months.

Sampling procedures prohibit such a broad generalization. The research report implies the conclusion can be applied to *all* users of online dating services, when the research studied only one online Web site and only a total of 229 people. The study fails to describe how the sample was selected; hence, the randomness and breadth for this site are unknown. It is quite possible, for example, that those who volunteered to participate were those who had been most successful in finding a good match. The research report is flawed because it greatly overgeneralizes.

Attention: *We can generalize only to people and events that are like those that we have studied in the research.*

BIASED SURVEYS AND QUESTIONNAIRES

It's early evening. You have just finished dinner. The phone rings. "We're conducting a survey of public opinion. Will you answer a few questions?" If you answer "yes," you will be among thousands who annually take part in surveys—one of the research methods you will encounter most frequently. Think how often you hear the phrase "according to recent polls."

Surveys and questionnaires are usually used to measure people's behavior, attitudes, and beliefs. Just how dependable are they? It depends! Survey responses are subject to many influences; So, one has to be very cautious in interpreting their meaning. Let's examine some of these influences.

First, for survey responses to be meaningful, they must be answered honestly. That is, verbal reports need to mirror actual beliefs and attitudes. Yet, for many reasons, people frequently shade the truth. For example, they may give answers they think they ought to give, rather than answers that reflect their true beliefs. They may experience hostility toward the questionnaire or toward the kind of question asked. They may give too little thought to the question. If you have ever been a survey participant, you can probably think of other influences.

Attention: *You cannot assume that survey responses accurately reflect true attitudes.*

Second, many survey questions are ambiguous in their wording; the questions are subject to multiple interpretations. Different individuals may in essence be responding to different questions! For example, imagine the multiple possible interpretations of the following survey question: "Do you think there is quality programming on television?" The more ambiguous the wording of a survey, the less credibility you can place in the results.

You should always ask the question, "How were the survey questions worded?" Usually, the more specifically a question is worded, the more likely that different individuals will interpret it similarly.

Third, surveys contain many *built-in biases* that make them even more suspect. Two of the most important are *biased wording* and *biased context.* Biased wording of a question is a common problem; a small change in how a question is asked can have a major effect on how a question is answered. Let's examine a conclusion based on a recent poll and then look at the survey question.

> A college professor found that 56 percent of respondents attending his university believe that the Obama healthcare program is a major mistake for the country.

Now look closely at the survey question: "What do you think about the president's misguided efforts to impose Obamacare socialism on the nation?" Do you see the built-in bias? The "leading" words are "the president's misguided efforts" and "impose Obamacare socialism." Wouldn't the responses have been quite different if the question had read, "What do you think about the president's attempt to provide a health care system that will provide expanded coverage, lower costs, and increased health care coverage to Americans?" Thus, the responses obtained here are a distorted indicator of attitudes concerning the new healthcare program.

Survey and questionnaire data must always be examined for possible bias. *Look carefully at the wording of the questions!*

The effect of *context* on an answer to a question can also be powerful. Even answers to identical questions can vary from poll to poll depending on how the questionnaire is presented and how the question is embedded in the survey. The following question was included in two recent surveys: "Do you think we should lower the drinking age from 21?" In one survey, the question was preceded by another question: "Do you think the right to vote should be given to children at the age of 18 as it currently is?" In the other survey, no preceding question occurred. Not surprisingly, the two surveys showed different results. Can you see how the context might have affected respondents?

Another important contextual factor is *length*. In long surveys, people may respond differently to later items than to earlier items simply because they get tired. *Be alert to contextual factors when evaluating survey results.*

Because the way people respond to surveys is affected by many unknown factors, such as the need to please the interviewer or the interpretation of the question, should we ever treat survey evidence as good evidence? There are heated debates about this issue, but our answer is "yes," as long as we are careful and do not generalize further than warranted. Some surveys are more reputable than others. The better the quality of the survey, the more you should be influenced by its results.

Our recommendation is to examine survey *procedures* carefully before accepting survey *results*. Once you have ascertained the quality of the procedures, you can choose to generate your own *qualified generalization*—one that takes into account any biases you might find. Even biased surveys can be informative; but you need to know the biases in order to not be unduly persuaded by the findings.

CRITICAL EVALUATION OF A RESEARCH-BASED ARGUMENT

Let's now use our questions about research to evaluate the following argument in which research evidence has been used to support a conclusion.

> It is time to abolish tenure in the public school system according to a *Time* Magazine poll, which asked Americans what they think of the current state of public education. Among the questions the survey addressed was the following: How can policy be changed to make the public-education system better? The following reported results showed a major discontent of the American public with the tenure system: 28% of those surveyed support the current system of tenure for teachers, which makes it difficult to remove them from their jobs; and 56% think tenured long-time teachers are not motivated to work hard.
>
> The poll was conducted by telephone in August of 2010 among a national random sample of 1,000 Americans aged 18 and older.

How good is the evidence? The research is presented here in an uncritical fashion. We see no sign of strong-sense critical thinking. The report makes no references to special strengths or weaknesses of the study, although it does provide some brief detail about the sampling procedures so that we can speculate about its worth as the basis of a generalization. There is no indication of whether the study has been replicated or how it fits into a broader context of studies about what is needed to improve public education. We do not know what benefits publishing these findings may have had for the person making the argument.

Is there any evidence of overgeneralizing? The sample is relatively large and is described as random, two strengths. The survey was done by telephone, however; and thus we don't know what kinds of selective factors led to people choosing to take part in the survey. Also, we don't know whether cell phones were used; so participation may be biased against "cell phone only" people. It is impossible to determine sampling breadth because we don't know what aspects of the general population were represented by the responses to the phone calling. For example, were some areas of the country, some occupations, or some age groups more represented than others? More information about how the survey was introduced and described to those called and characteristics of those who volunteered would be helpful. Could there have been a bias in those willing to cooperate with the callers? Such questions suggest that we should be wary of overgeneralizing from these results.

Are the survey questions biased? The argument omits the specific wording of the questions used for the two findings and also fails to list other questions included in the survey; so we can't determine what kinds of order or context biasing effects might be present. The phrase "which makes it difficult to remove them from their jobs" highlights a negative aspect of tenure, suggesting that the question asked was a question loaded against tenure.

We have raised enough questions about the given passage to be wary of the generalizability of its factual claims. We would want to a close look at the entire research study and also rely on much more related research before we could conclude that these claims are dependable.

Let's now look at a very different source of evidence.

ANALOGIES AS EVIDENCE

Look closely at the structure of the following brief arguments, paying special attention to the reason supporting the conclusion.

> There is no need to fear that the Internet will lead to the disappearance of newspapers and magazines. After all, TV dinners didn't make cooking disappear.
>
> As an educator, it is important to weed out problem students early and take care of the problems they present because one bad egg ruins the omelet.

Both arguments use *analogies* as evidence, a very different kind of evidence from what we have previously been evaluating. At first glance, analogies often seem very persuasive. But they often deceive us; and we need to ask, "How do we decide whether an analogy is good evidence?" Before reading on, try to determine the persuasiveness of the above-mentioned two arguments.

Did you note that the analogies involve comparisons? They rely on *resemblance* as the major form of evidence. The reasoning is as follows: "We know a lot about something in our world (X), and another event of interest (Y) seems to be *like* X in some important way. If these two things are alike in one or more respects, then they will probably be alike in other respects as well."

For example, when people get depressed, many psychiatrists treat the depressive behavior as a form of mental disease because they see the behavior as having important similarities to having a physical illness, and thus they treat the person with antidepressant medications. They see the mental problems like a *symptom* of a physical disorder. If they were to see the behavior as "experiencing a problem in living," they might treat the patient very differently. We reason in a similar fashion when we choose to buy a CD because a friend recommends it. We reason that because we resemble each other in a number of likes and dislikes, we will enjoy the same music.

An argument that uses a well-known similarity between two things as the basis for a conclusion about a relatively unknown characteristic of one of those things is an *argument by analogy*.

Analogies both stimulate insights and deceive us. For example, analogies have been highly productive in scientific and legal reasoning. When we infer conclusions about humans on the basis of research with mice, we reason by analogy. Much of our thinking about the structure of the atom is analogical reasoning. When we make a decision in a legal case, we may base that decision on the similarity of that case to preceding cases. For example, when judges approach the question of whether restricting corporate contributions to political candidates violates the constitutional protection of free speech and freedom of expression, they must decide whether financial contributions are analogous to freedom of speech; thus, they reason by analogy. Such reasoning can be quite insightful and persuasive.

Identifying and Comprehending Analogies

You can identify an argument by analogy by noticing that something that has well-known characteristics is being used to help explain something that has some similar characteristics. In doing so, the assumption is being made that if the event we're interested in explaining is like the event to which it is being compared in important ways, it will be like that event in other important ways.

For example, consider the analogy, "Relearning geometry is like riding a bike. Once you start, it all comes back to you." Riding a bicycle, an activity with well-known characteristics, is used to explain relearning geometry, the unknown, which is an activity with some, but not all, similar characteristics.

We are familiar with the idea of getting on a bike after a period of time and "it all coming back to us" as we start to ride again. The analogy, therefore, explains relearning geometry in the same way, arguing if one starts to do geometry problems, remembering how to do such problems will simply come back to the person. Note that we started with a similarity—both activities involve learning a skill—and assumed that therefore they would have other important similarities.

Once the nature and structure of analogies is understood, you should be able to identify analogies in arguments. It is especially important to identify analogies when they are used to set the tone of the conversation. Such analogies are used to "frame" an argument. To identify framing analogies, look for comparisons that are used to not only explain a point, but also to influence the direction a discussion will take.

For example, in the 2004 presidential election, the war in Iraq was an important issue. Opponents of the war used the analogy comparing the war in Iraq to the Vietnam War. The analogy was not only an attempt to explain what is happening in Iraq now, but also to cause people to look negatively upon the war in Iraq. Conversely, proponents of the war in Iraq used the analogy comparing the war to World War II. World War II carries with it more positive connotations than does the Vietnam War, so this analogy was used to reframe the discussion in terms more favorable to the war in Iraq. Always look for comparisons that attempt to direct the reaction to an object through framing. A careful evaluation of framing analogies will prevent you from being misled by a potentially deceptive analogy.

Framing analogies is not the only thing to be wary of when looking for analogies in arguments. One must also be careful when evaluating arguments that use overly emotional comparisons. For example, some politicians in arguing against the recent health care bill compared end-of-life planning to death panels. Who could possibly be in favor of a bill that called for death panels? Overly emotional analogies cloud the real issues in arguments and prevent substantive discourse. Try to identify comparisons made that contain significant emotional connotations to avoid being deceived by these analogies.

Evaluating Analogies

Because analogical reasoning is so common and has the potential to be both persuasive and faulty, you will find it very useful to recognize such reasoning and know how to systematically evaluate it. To evaluate the quality of an analogy, you need to focus on two factors.

1. The ways the two things being compared are similar and different.
2. The *relevance* of the similarities and the differences.

A word of caution: You can almost always find SOME similarities between any two things. So, analogical reasoning will not be persuasive simply because of many similarities. Strong analogies will be ones in which the two things we compare possess *relevant* similarities and lack *relevant* differences. All analogies try to illustrate underlying principles. *Relevant similarities and differences are ones that directly relate to the underlying principle illustrated by the analogy.*

Let's check out the soundness of the following argument by analogy.

> I do not allow my dog to run around the neighborhood getting into trouble, so why shouldn't I enforce an 8 o'clock curfew on my 16-year-old? I am responsible for keeping my daughter safe, as well as responsible for what she might do when she is out. My dog stays in the yard, and I want my daughter to stay in the house. This way, I know exactly what both are doing.

A major similarity between a pet and a child is that both are thought of as not being full citizens with all the rights and responsibilities of adults. Plus, as the speaker asserts, he is responsible for keeping his dog and daughter safe. We note some relevant differences, however. A dog is a pet that lacks higher order thinking skills and cannot assess right and wrong. A daughter, however, is a human being with the cognitive capacity to tell when things are right and wrong and when she should not do something that might get her (or her parents) in trouble. Also, as a human, she has certain rights and deserves a certain amount of respect for her autonomy. Thus, because a daughter can do things a dog cannot, the differences are relevant in assessing the analogy. The failure of the analogy to allow for the above-listed distinctions causes it to fail to provide strong support for the conclusion.

Another strategy that may help you evaluate reasoning by analogy is to *generate alternative analogies* for understanding the same phenomenon that the author or speaker is trying to understand. Such analogies may either support or contradict the conclusions inferred from the original analogy. If they contradict the conclusion, they then reveal problems in the initial reasoning by analogy.

A productive way to generate your own analogies is the following:

1. Identify some important features of what you are studying.
2. Try to identify other situations with which you are familiar that have some similar features. Brainstorm. Try to imagine diverse situations.
3. Try to determine whether the familiar situation can provide you with some insights about the unfamiliar situation.

For example, in thinking about pornography, you could try to think of other situations in which people repeatedly think something is demeaning because of the way people are treated in a given situation, or because of what watching something might cause others to do. Do segregation, racist/sexist jokes, or employment discrimination come to mind? How about arguments that claim playing violent video games, watching action movies, or listening to heavy metal music cause children to act violently? Do such arguments trigger other ways to think about pornography?

You should now be capable of systematically evaluating the two brief analogical arguments at the beginning of this section. Ask the questions you need to ask to recognize an argument by analogy. Then, ask the questions to evaluate the argument. Look for relevant similarities and differences. Usually, the greater the proportion of relevant similarities to relevant differences, the stronger the analogy. An analogy is especially compelling when you can find *no* relevant difference and you can find good evidence that the relevant similarities do indeed exist.

We found a relevant difference that weakens each of our two initial sample analogies. Check your evaluation against our list.

> (First example) Both TV dinners and the Internet made it quicker and easier to accomplish complex time-consuming tasks. Reading magazines and newspapers, however, may not provide the same kind of pleasure as cooking a gourmet meal.
>
> (Second example) The interactions of students in a classroom environment are very complex. The effect any one student might have on the group cannot easily be determined, just as the effects the group might have on the individual are difficult to predict. Conversely, a rotten egg will definitely spoil any food made from it. Also, it is problematic to think of people as unchanging objects, such as rotten eggs, that have no potential for growth and change.

Analogies that trick or deceive us fit our definition of a reasoning fallacy; such deception is called the *faulty analogy fallacy*.

Fallacy: Faulty Analogy: Occurs when an analogy is proposed in which there are important relevant dissimilarities.

In one sense, all analogies are faulty because they make the mistaken assumption that because two things are alike in one or more respects, they are necessarily alike in some other important respect. It is probably best for you to think of analogies as varying from very weak to very strong. But even the best analogies are only suggestive. Thus, if an author draws a conclusion about one case from a comparison to another case, then she should provide further evidence to support the principle revealed by the most significant similarity.

USING EVIDENCE IN YOUR OWN WRITING

To help you improve the quality of evidence in your own writing, we have a suggestion.

When conducting your own research, you need to observe and record consistently. Before starting an independent research, a researcher develops a set of procedures or rules to guide the process. The formal name for these procedures is *methodology*. When you carefully decide on a methodology, you often preemptively avoid problems we discussed earlier in this chapter, such as biased questionnaires and sampling issues.

Another aspect of conducting your own research is keeping accurate and available records. Our memories are fallible and prone to make errors when we try to recall what we have seen and heard. Technology, however, has created some very useful tools to address this concern. You can video or audio record interviews or observations. You can use Web-based survey tools. Remember you should always date your observations, surveys, or interviews, and you should keep them organized either electronically or with hard copies. Your readers should be able to look over your findings. You may even want to return to them for other projects.

Lastly, keep in mind the limitations of your findings. We discussed the risk of overgeneralization earlier in the chapter. If you incorporate your own research into your writing projects, this concern applies especially to you. The implications of your research are limited to the regions you surveyed or observed. If you seek to demonstrate that your findings have far-reaching implications, you may want to supplement your writing with other authors' findings.

Research and the Internet

It's the 21st century. We suspect that you are light-years ahead of technological half-wits like Homer Simpson, who marveled, "They have the Internet on computers, now?" We'd be surprised if you were not taking advantage of the Internet when you prepare to write. Internet research has fundamentally changed evidence gathering for most of us, making information exponentially more accessible. What's the trade-off for this unprecedented level of availability? We have to consider the evidence we gather with even greater scrutiny. Keep these tips in mind to help you address the particular difficulties that arise with Internet research.

Earlier in this chapter, we discussed the importance of investigating an author's background. We urged you to determine potential biases or conflicts of interests. To weigh the opinion of an authority, we need to know that person's credentials and potential biases. The *Onion*, the popular satirical news site, illustrates how the Internet makes this task particular difficult. In its 2008 mock article "Local Idiot to Post Comment on Internet," it quotes the "local idiot" as he divulges his plans: "Later this evening, I intend to watch the video in question, click the 'reply' link above the box reserved for user comments, and draft a response, being careful to put as little thought into it as possible, while making sure to use all capital letters and incorrect punctuation [. . .]. Although I do not yet know exactly what my comment will entail, I can say with a great degree of certainty that it will be incredibly stupid." If only all contributors to the Internet were so forthright!

The importance of investigating a source's credibility is even greater when we add Internet sources to the equation. The Internet often draws comparisons to the Wild West. There is no sheriff in town making sure that only true and fair statements are published by respective folk. In its current form, it is relatively unrestricted. Anyone can create a Web page or a blog. Web pages can appear to look trustworthy when they are actually published by someone with a hidden agenda. Take a look at some of the Web sites created by the social activists known as The Yes Men, such as http://www.dowethics.com, a site they created to look and sound like the real deal. Upon investigation, visitors to the site discovered that it was not created by Dow. In fact, the site was a biting critique of the chemical company's environmental practices. While this example is unusual, we hope it reminds you that the creators of a Web site may have a political, commercial, or even artistic agenda that is not readily apparent.

Even after you decide that Web-based author is reliable, you should ask more questions. Because the Web does not have a sheriff, evidence that is questionable or untrue can easily be posted. Comedy Central's satirical pundit Stephen Colbert wanted to demonstrate how easily false information can be posted on the Internet. In one episode of his Colbert Report, he edited the public Internet encyclopedia Wikipedia. For five hours, Wikipedia entries stated that George Washington did NOT own slaves and the population of African elephants tripled in the previous six months. (For another satire of this very real concern, check out the *Onion*'s 2002 article "Factual Error Found on Internet," which begins "The Information Age was dealt a stunning blow Monday, when a factual error was discovered on the Internet."). To combat this problem, avoid writing about evidence that has not been credited to a specific source. Take the time to look up the original source. When a snippet of another article is posted or cited, the author who posted the snippet may have misunderstood or taken the information out of context.

PRACTICE EXERCISES

Critical Question: ***How good is the evidence?***

Evaluate each of these practice passages by examining the quality of the evidence provided.

Passage 1

Are children of alcoholics more likely to be alcoholics themselves? In answering the question, researchers sampled 451 people in Alcoholics Anonymous to see how many would say that one, or both, of their parents were alcoholics. People in AA used in the study currently attend AA somewhere in Ohio, Michigan, or Indiana and were asked by people in charge of the local AA programs to volunteer to fill out a survey. The research found that 77 percent of the respondents had at least one parent they classified as an alcoholic. The study also surveyed 451 people randomly from the same states who claim not to be heavy drinkers. Of the nonheavy drinkers, 23 percent would label at least one of their parents as alcoholic.

Passage 2

Why shouldn't law students taking a difficult exam be permitted to use their laptop computers? Attorneys can use their computers to look up information relevant to difficult cases.

Passage 3

One of the greatest symbols of the United States is the American flag. While cases in the past have defended desecration of the flag as symbolic speech, I argue, "Where is the speech in such acts?" If you have something bad to say about the United States, say it, but do not cheapen the flag with your actions. Many Americans died to keep that flag flying.

Those who want to support flag burning and other such despicable acts are outnumbered. Last month, 75 people were surveyed in a restaurant in Dallas, Texas, and were asked if they supported the unpatriotic desecration of the American flag in an attempt to express some sort of anti-American idea. Ninety-three percent responded that they were not in favor of desecration of the American flag. Therefore, our national lawmakers should pass a law protecting the American flag against such horrible actions.

Sample Responses

Passage 1

CONCLUSION: *Children of alcoholics are more likely to become alcoholics than are children of nonalcoholics.*

REASON: *More alcoholics than nonalcoholics reported having at least one alcoholic parent.*

Note that the results presented are from one study without reference to how typical these results are. We also do not know where this information was published, so we can make no assessments regarding how rigorously the study was reviewed before publication. However, we can ask some useful questions about the study. The sample size is quite large, but its breadth is questionable. Although multiple states were sampled, to what extent are the people in the AA programs in these states typical of alcoholics across the nation? Also, how do alcoholics in AA compare to alcoholics who have not sought help? Perhaps the most important sampling problem was the lack of a random sample. While the self-reported nonalcoholics were randomly selected in the three states, the respondents in AA were selected on a voluntary basis.

Do those who volunteered to talk about their parents differ greatly from those who did not volunteer? If there is a difference between the volunteers and nonvolunteers, then the sample is biased.

How accurate are the rating measurements? First, no definition for *alcoholic* is given beyond those answering the survey currently being in AA. In addition, we are not told of any criteria given to the research participants for rating parents as alcoholic. Thus, we are uncertain of the accuracy of the judgments about whether someone was an alcoholic. Also, problematic is the fact that the selection of the supposed control group of nonalcoholics is based on self-assessment. We know that there is a socially acceptable answer of not being an alcoholic, and people tend to give socially acceptable answers when they know them. This response tendency could also bias the sampling in the supposed control group. We would want to know more about the accuracy of these ratings before we could have much confidence in the conclusion.

Passage 2

CONCLUSION: *Students taking exams should be able to use their laptops.*

REASON: *Students using the laptop to look up answers on difficult exams is like attorneys being able to use laptops to find answers to difficult cases.*

First we note that the reasoning is based on a comparison. Something we are familiar with, attorneys using their laptops to help with difficult cases, is used to help better understand an event that is similar in some ways: Both situations involve using laptops to look up answers to difficult problems. A significant difference, however, is that students taking an exam are being tested for knowledge that they are supposed to possess without external help. This difference is sufficient for us to reject the analogy as proof for the conclusion.

CHAPTER

9

Are There Rival Causes?

We begin this chapter with a story.

> An inquisitive little boy noticed that the sun would show up in the sky in the morning and disappear at night. Puzzled by where the sun went, the boy tried to watch the sunset really closely. However, he still could not figure out where the sun was going. Then, the boy also noticed that his babysitter showed up in the mornings and left at night. One day, he asked his babysitter where she went at night. The babysitter responded, "I go home." Linking his babysitter's arrival and departure with the coming of day and night, he concluded that his babysitter's leaving caused the sun to also go home.

This story clearly illustrates a common difficulty in the use of evidence: trying to figure out what caused something to happen. We cannot determine an intelligent approach to avoiding a problem or encouraging a particular positive outcome until we understand the causal pattern that gave rise to the phenomenon in the first place. For example, we want to know what caused the financial crisis of 2008. Or, *why* has the rate of obesity been increasing so markedly over the last 10 years.

The story also shows a very common difficulty in using evidence to prove that something caused something else—the problem of *rival causes*. The fictional little boy offered one interpretation of his observations: "The sun sets at night because my babysitter goes home." We expect that you can see another very plausible explanation for why the sun sets.

Although rival causes will rarely be as obvious as they are in our story, you will frequently encounter experts presenting one hypothesis to explain events or research findings when other plausible hypotheses could also explain them. Usually, these experts will not reveal rival causes to you because they do not want you to detract from the sound of certainty associated with their claims; you will have to produce them. Doing so can be especially helpful as you decide, "How good is the evidence?" The existence of multiple, plausible rival causes for events reduces our confidence in the cause originally offered by the author.

Critical Question: ***Are there rival causes?***

Attention: *A rival cause is a plausible alternative explanation that can explain why a certain outcome occurred.*

WHEN TO LOOK FOR RIVAL CAUSES

You need to look for rival causes when you have good reason to believe that the writer or speaker is using evidence to support a claim about the cause of something. The word *cause* means "to bring about, make happen, or affect." Communicators can indicate causal thinking to you in a number of ways. We have listed a few.

EXHIBIT 9-1 Indicators of Causal Relations

✓ X leads to . . .	✓ X increases the likelihood . . .
✓ X influences . . .	✓ X determines . . .
✓ X is linked to . . .	✓ X is associated with . . .
✓ X deters . . .	✓ X has the effect of . . .

These clues to causal thinking should help you recognize when a communicator is making a causal claim. Once you note such a claim, be alert to the possibility of rival causes.

THE PERVASIVENESS OF RIVAL CAUSES

Detecting rival causes can help us better react to causal conclusions encountered in (a) our everyday personal relationships, (b) past or ongoing world events, and (c) results of research studies.

Following are several examples.

Example 1. Reasoning in interpersonal relationships.

College student talking to a friend: It's been over 24 hours and my boyfriend hasn't returned my text message. He must be mad at me.

Rival causes: Maybe he's busy studying for a test, or perhaps he has misplaced his cell phone.

Example 2. A major world event.

On the afternoon of November 5, 2009, a mass murder took place at Fort Hood, a large military installation in Texas. A psychiatrist named Nadil Malik Hasan entered his workplace, the Soldier Readiness Center, where personnel receive routine medical treatment immediately and prior to deployment; then, reports say that after taking a seat and bowing his head, he stood up and shot and killed 13 people while wounding 30 others. Observers reported that he used two handguns and seemed to focus on soldiers in uniform.

As is typically the case following such violent acts, attempts have been made to understand such behavior, and much debate about the causes has emerged. Rival causes have included:

1. Islamic terrorism. Hasan was described as a devout Muslin who had a history of contacts with Muslin extremists who had been investigated by the FBI for possible terrorist activities.
2. A psychological stress reaction, triggered by Hasan's deployment to Afghanistan on November 28. He had been encountering evidence of the bad conditions of returning soldiers on a daily basis and was too shaken up by these stories to function properly. According to a relative, "deployment overseas was his worst nightmare."
3. An overreaction to a workplace event. Hasan's superior refused to process his requests that some of his patients be prosecuted for war crimes based on statements they made during psychiatric sessions with him.
4. Political correctness. Hasan had shown many signs of mental disturbance and had demonstrated proterrorist leanings; these were ignored in the desire to protect diversity.

Example 3. A research study.

A recent study suggests that breast-feeding benefits mothers as well as babies. The study found that women who had breast-fed for more than a year in their entire lifetimes were almost 10 percent less likely to have had a heart attack or a stroke in their postmenopausal years than those who had never breast-fed. They were also less likely to have diabetes, hypertension, and high cholesterol. The research, published in the May issue of the journal *Obstetrics & Gynecology*, analyzed data on some 139,681 women who had enrolled in the Women's Health Initiative, a long-term national study of postmenopausal women.

In this study, the researcher probably began with the hypothesis that breast-feeding *causes* health benefits for mothers, and she found evidence consistent with this hypothesis. But let us offer different, or rival, causes for the same findings.

1. Women who breast-feed may simply on average lead more healthful lives than those who do not. For example, they may exercise more, or eat differently, than women who do not breast-feed.
2. Women who choose not to breast-feed may work outside the home more hours, possibly causing more life stress and thus incurring more health problems.
3. Reasons that women reject breast-feeding may be related to having more health problems than those who choose to breast-feed. For example, mothers who are taking medications or are smokers may be concerned about the safety of breast-feeding.

Lessons Learned

1. Many kinds of events are open to explanation by rival causes.
2. Experts can examine the same evidence and discover different causes to explain it.
3. Most communicators will provide you with only their favored causes; the critical reader or listener must generate rival causes.
4. Generating rival causes is a creative process; usually, such causes will not be obvious.
5. Finally, the certainty of a particular causal claim is inversely related to the number of plausible rival causes. Hence, identifying the multiple rival causes gives the critical thinker the proper sense of intellectual humility.

In the following sections, we explore the implications of these lessons for the critical thinker.

DETECTING RIVAL CAUSES

Locating rival causes is much like being a good detective. When you recognize situations in which rival causes are possible, you want to ask yourself questions like:

? Can I think of any other way to interpret the evidence?
? What else might have caused this act or these findings?
? If I looked at this from another point of view, what might I see as important causes?
? If this interpretation is incorrect, what other interpretation might make sense?

THE CAUSE OR *A* CAUSE

There is an alarming increase in the rate of depression among elementary aged children. Talk show hosts begin to interview the experts about *the* cause.

It is genetic. It is the prevalence of teasing among peer groups. It is parental neglect. It is too much TV news coverage of terrorism and wars. It is lack of religion. It is stress. The experts may *claim* to have the answer, but they are not likely to *know* it. That is because a frequently made error is to look for a simple, single cause of an event when "the" cause is really the result of a combination of many *contributory* causes—causes that help to create a total set of conditions necessary for the event to occur. For example, the impetus to commit mass murder likely results from unique combinations of many contributory causes.

Multiple contributory causes occur more often than do single causes in situations involving the characteristics or activities of humans. The best causal explanation is often one that combines many causes that *only together* are sufficient to bring about the event. So, the best answer experts can give to the talk show hosts' question is, "We don't know *the* cause for such events, but we can speculate about possible causes that might have contributed to the event." Thus, when we are searching for rival causes, we need to remember that any single cause that we identify is much more likely to be a contributory cause than *the* cause.

When communicators fail to consider the complexity of causes, they commit the *causal oversimplication fallacy*.

Fallacy: Causal Oversimplification: Explaining an event by relying on causal factors that are insufficient to account for the event or by overemphasizing the role of one or more of these factors.

In some sense, almost all causal explanations are oversimplifications; therefore, you have to be fair to communicators who offer explanations that do not include *every* possible cause of an event. Causal conclusions, however, should include sufficient causal factors to convince you that they are not too greatly oversimplified, or the author should make clear to you that the causal factor she emphasizes in her conclusion is only one of a number of possible contributing causes—**a** cause, not **the** cause.

RIVAL CAUSES FOR DIFFERENCES BETWEEN GROUPS

One of the most common ways for researchers to try to find a cause for some event is to *compare groups, as was the case in the study about breast-feeding mentioned earlier*. For example, you will frequently encounter the following kinds of references to group comparisons:

Researchers compared an experimental group to a control group.
One group received treatment X; the other group didn't.
A group with learning disabilities was compared with a group without learning disabilities.

When researchers find such differences between groups, they often conclude, "Those differences support my hypothesis." For example, a researcher might find that a group of back-pain sufferers who treated their pain with a new drug report experiencing less pain than a group with back pain that did not use that drug. She then concludes that the use of that drug caused the difference. The problem is that *research groups almost always differ in more than one important way*, and thus group differences often are consistent with multiple causes. Therefore, when you see communicators use findings of differences between groups to support one cause, always ask, "Are there rival causes that might also explain the differences in the groups?"

Let's take a look at a study that compares groups and try to detect rival causes.

> In a recent research study, students who prepared for a standardized test by taking a special course designed to teach students how to take the test scored higher than students who prepared for the same standardized test by reviewing several books about the test.

The question we need to ask is, "How might these two groups have differed in important ways other than the test preparation they experienced?" Did you think of either of the following possible important differences between the two groups that might account for test score differences?

- *Differences in students' academic (and economic) background.* Maybe the course is expensive, and only those students who had the money could afford to take it. Moreover, perhaps those students who could afford the class also could afford better private school education before taking the test and thus started from a privileged position in comparison with the students who did not take the class.
- *Differences in motivation.* Perhaps the students who signed up for the class are the students who really want to excel in the test. Students who read a few books might be less interested in scoring really well on the standardized test. Alternatively, the students might have chosen study methods based on how they best learn. Those who learn best in a class setting might be predisposed to do well on standardized tests.

You probably came up with other important differences. *Remember:* Many factors can cause research groups to differ!

Being aware that some ways to compare groups are far superior to others in minimizing the number of rival causes is helpful. Acquainting you with the pros and cons of all research designs is beyond the scope of *Asking the Right Questions*, but we want to encourage you to acquaint yourselves with various research designs while helping you spot the design that experts agree is the best between-groups design to minimize rival causes—*the randomized experimental design.* This design, often called the gold standard, compares how one group responds to an experimental intervention, such as a drug treatment, against how an identical group behaves without the intervention.

This design minimizes rival causes; so you should have increased confidence in causal conclusions supported by such a research approach. *Look for reference to this design when you are evaluating the results of between groups studies.*

Online help: For a more in-depth explanation of the benefits of randomized experimental designs over other between-groups research designs, see http://www.pearsonhighered.com/browne, Chapter 9.

CONFUSING CAUSATION WITH ASSOCIATION

We have an inherent tendency to "see" events that are associated, or that "go together," as events that cause one another. That is, we conclude that because characteristic X (e.g., amount of energy bars consumed) is associated with characteristic Y (e.g., performance in an athletic event), X causes Y. Here is another example of such reasoning:

> Have you noticed that as hip hop music has become more popular, fewer of our youth are attending church? Such music is causing a breakdown in the moral fiber of our youth.

When we think this way, we are, however, often very wrong! Why? Usually multiple hypotheses can explain why X and Y "go together." In fact, there are at least four different kinds of hypotheses to account for any such relationship. Knowing what these are will help you discover rival causes. Let's illustrate each of the four with a research example.

> A recent study reported that "smoking combats flu." The researchers studied 525 smokers and found that 67 percent of the smokers did not have the flu once over the last three years and hypothesized that the nicotine in the smoke from cigarettes destroys the flu virus before it can spread and cause sickness.

Before people who are feeling sick start smoking to prevent the onset of the flu, they should consider each of the following four potential explanations for the research findings.

Explanation 1: *X is a cause of Y.* (Smoking does indeed kill the flu virus.)

Explanation 2: *Y is a cause of X.* (Being free from viruses makes it more likely that people will keep smoking.)

Explanation 3: *X and Y are associated because of some third factor, Z.* (Smoking and being without the flu are both caused by related factors, such as frequent washing of the hands after smoking prevents the spread of the flu virus.)

Explanation 4: *X and Y influence each other.* (People who do not usually catch the flu have a tendency to smoke, and the smoke may affect some potential illnesses.)

Remember: Association or correlation does not prove causation!

Yet most evidence used to prove causation is based only on association or correlation. When an author supports a hypothesis by pointing to an association between characteristics, always ask, "Are there other causes that explain the association?" Test yourself on the following study.

> A recent study reported that "ice cream causes crime." Researchers studied ice cream sales and crime rates over the last five years in the ten largest U.S. cities and found that as ice cream sales increase, so does the crime rate. They hypothesized that eating ice cream triggers a chemical reaction in one's brain an inclination toward crime.

We hope you can now see that ice cream eaters need not be concerned that they are about to commit a crime. What rival causes did you think of? Couldn't the increased summer heat account for the association between ice cream sales (X) and crime (Y)?

This confusion between correlation and causation is as understandable as it is dangerous. A cause will indeed precede its effect. But many things preceded that effect. Most of them were not causal.

You should now be able to identify two common causal reasoning fallacies, *confusion of cause and effect fallacy* and *neglect of a common cause fallacy*, by attending to the above-mentioned four possible explanations of why events might be associated:

Fallacy: Confusion of Cause and Effect: Confusing the cause with the effect of an event or failing to recognize that the two events may be influencing each other.

Fallacy: Neglect of a Common Cause: Failure to recognize that two events may be related because of the effects of a common third factor.

CONFUSING "AFTER THIS" WITH "BECAUSE OF THIS"

Shortly after being featured on the cover of *Sports Illustrated*, the quarterback for the Chicago Bears, Jake Cutler, was injured early in the championship game of the National Football League, and the Bears lost to the Green Bay Packers, 31–17. Had the dreaded *Sports Illustrated* cover jinx—the belief that being on the cover of *Sports Illustrated* leads to bad luck—struck again, or might there be other causal explanations for the quarterback's bad luck? We think you can see many other rival causes for the downfall of Cutler and the Bears, such as the defense of the Packers.

Often, we try to explain a particular event as follows: Because event B *followed* event A, then event A *caused* event B. Such reasoning occurs because human beings have a strong tendency to believe that if two events occur close together in time, the first one must have caused the second one.

Many events that occur after other events in time are not caused by the preceding events. When we wrongly conclude that the first event causes the second because it preceded it, we commit the *post hoc, ergo propter hoc* (meaning: "after this, therefore because of this") *fallacy*, or, for short, the *post hoc fallacy*. Such reasoning is responsible for many superstitious beliefs, such as the *Sports Illustrated* cover jinx. For example, you may have written an excellent paper while wearing a particular hat, so now you always insist on wearing the same hat when you write papers.

Fallacy: Post Hoc: Assuming that a particular event, B, is caused by another event, A, simply because B follows A in time.

The following examples further illustrate the problem with this kind of reasoning.

> "The quarter I found yesterday must be lucky. Since I have found it, I got an A on a really hard test, my least favorite class was canceled, and my favorite movie was on TV last night." (Never mind the fact that I studied really hard for my test, my professor has a 6-year-old who recently had the flu, and the TV schedule is made far in advance of my finding a quarter.)

As you might guess, political and business leaders are fond of using the post hoc argument, especially when it works in their favor. For example, they tend to take credit for anything good that takes place after they assumed their leadership role and to place blame elsewhere for anything bad that happens.

Remember: The finding that one event follows another in time does not by itself prove causation; it may be only a coincidence. When you see such reasoning, always ask yourself, "Are there rival causes that could account for the event?" and, "Is there any good evidence other than the fact that one event followed the other event in time?"

EXPLAINING INDIVIDUAL EVENTS OR ACTS

What caused the 2010 volcanic eruptions in Iceland? Why is Facebook so popular? Why did the Tea Party become so influential in the 2010 Congressional election?

Like our question about the Fort Hood massacre, these questions seek explanations of individual historical events. First, as we saw in the Fort Hood case, so many different stories for the same event can make sense. Second, the way we explain events is greatly influenced by social and political forces, as well as by individual psychological perspectives regarding beliefs.

For example, men view the cause of drug abuse differently than women, Democrats might view the causes of poverty differently from Republicans, and biologists might view the causes of depression differently than psychologists or sociologists.

Also, a common bias is the *fundamental attribution error*, in which we typically overestimate the importance of personal tendencies relative to situational factors in interpreting the behavior of others. That is, we tend to see the cause of other's behavior as coming from within (their personal characteristics) rather than from without (situational forces.) So, for example, when people steal, we are likely to view the stealing initially as a result of their tendency to be immoral or to lack a conscience. However, we should also consider the role of outside circumstances such as poverty or peer pressure.

Another kind of common psychological error is to start with a limited number of possible causes and then to interpret additional information (even if it is irrelevant) as corroborating these existing hypotheses, rather than keeping the information separate or generating new, perhaps more complex, hypotheses. Our tendency is to simplify the world; yet, explanations often require much complexity. Explaining events is not as simple as frequently portrayed by guest experts on the popular talk shows.

A further major problem in constructing the causes of past events is that much evidence relies on the memories of people, and abundant research suggests that memories are often greatly distorted.

How can we know whether we have a "good" explanation of a particular event or set of events? We can never know for sure. But we can make some progress by asking critical questions.

Be wary of accepting the first interpretation of an event you encounter. Search for rival causes and try to compare their credibility. Consider other perspectives from which the event of interest might be viewed. Read multiple versions of events to help expand your viewpoints. We must accept the fact that *many* events do not have a simple explanation.

EVALUATING RIVAL CAUSES

The more plausible the rival causes that you come up with, the less faith you can have in the initial explanation offered, at least until further evidence has been considered. As a critical thinker, you have to assess as best you can how each of the alternative explanations fits the available evidence, trying to be sensitive to your personal biases.

EXHIBIT 9-2 In comparing causes, apply the following criteria

- ✓ Their logical soundess
- ✓ Their consistency with other knowledge that you have
- ✓ Their previous success in explaning or predicting events

RIVAL CAUSES AND YOUR OWN COMMUNICATION

Causal arguments are among the most difficult for writers to construct. You have to sift through a bunch of possible causes, some that are legitimate and others that are falsely attractive. Then you must show that an actual causal relationship exists. This problem is illustrated in a classic clip of PBS's *Sesame Street*, during which the Muppet Bert found Ernie holding a banana to his ear. Bert asked him about his peculiar behavior and Ernie responded, "Listen, Bert, I use this banana to keep the alligators away." An exacerbated Bert pointed out that there are no alligators on Sesame Street to which Ernie proudly replied, "Right. It's doing a good job, isn't it, Bert?" Ernie mistakenly reasoned that two simultaneous events were related.

After you prove that a relationship exists, you must then demonstrate that the relationship moves in the direction you suggest. That is, A caused B, not B caused A, or C caused both A and B. Or something else entirely—in J. K. Rowling's *Harry Potter* series, the author recreates the classic chicken and the egg riddle about causal direction as "Which came first, the phoenix or the flame?" Luna Lovegood, a whimsical friend of the main characters, answered correctly; "a circle has no beginning."

Lastly, you may want to demonstrate that the causal relationships you focused on explain the phenomenon better than the alternatives. This entire process can be overwhelming. We suggest you break it down into steps. The first of these steps involves some creative thinking.

Exploring Potential Causes

You start the writing process like any other argument. You decide on a particular issue that interests you. In this instance, you are looking for an issue that explores causality. Such an issue may mention the term *cause* explicitly, such as "What were the causes of AMC's *The Walking Dead*'s record breaking viewership on cable television?" or "What causes diseases to become resistant to treatment?" Similarly, the issue may explicitly use the term *effect*: "What are the likely effects to the Cleveland economy of LeBron James's decision to leave the city for the Miami Heat?"

Once you decide on an issue, your next step is to brainstorm potential answers to the question. The process can be a creative one. One excellent way to approach the task is to adopt the questioning attitude of an annoying 5-year-old. Keep asking *why*. Let's return to our example of AMC's *The Walking Dead* to demonstrate. Why did *The Walking Dead* break cable records? Well, maybe because 18- to 49-year-olds like zombies. Enter the 5-year-old's attitude: Why do they like zombies? How would you answer that question? What might our inner youngster ask next? "Why else?" 18- to 49-year-olds like action series. "Why else?" *The Walking Dead* filled a niche that no other network filled. "Why else?" The acting, writing, and directing were well executed. "Why else?" You get the picture. Your friends, classmates, and other people in your life can help you during the brainstorming stage. They might think of a cause that had not crossed your mind.

Narrowing Down Your List of Potential Causes

Once you have brainstormed possible causes or effects for a phenomenon, it is time for research. You can return to Chapters 7 and 8 for guidance for your evidence gathering. You should pay close attention to whether the article you are considering incorporating into your argument actually demonstrates a causal relationship. Headlines can mislead readers into thinking that a study proved causation when the original researchers did not demonstrate that fact. Consider what the CNN headline "Twinkie diet helps nutrition professor lose 27 pounds" suggests. Eating Twinkies causes people to lose weight! In fact, carefully counting calories probably caused the professor to lose 27 pounds, not Twinkies.

You should always demonstrate to your reader that you have not ignored alternative explanations. Maybe over the course of your research, you discovered that seemingly plausible explanations were not supported by the evidence. You should tell your reader as much.

PRACTICE EXERCISES

Each of the following examples provides an argument to support a causal claim. Try to generate rival causes for such claims. Then try to determine how much you have weakened the author's claim by knowledge of rival causes.

Passage 1

Oranges to combat the blues. Researchers have recently revealed that eating two oranges a day can help alleviate depression. Researchers studied 13 patients who had feelings of depression. After three weeks of eating two oranges a day, 9 of the 13 people reported improvement in their condition. The researchers hypothesize that the citric acid and vitamin C in oranges stimulate serotonin production, helping to combat depression.

Passage 2

Why did the corporate executive steal funds from his business? A close look at his life can provide a clear and convincing answer. The executive comes from a very successful family where his parents are doctors and his siblings are lawyers. As a corporate executive, he was not making as much money as his family members. Also, the executive believes heavily in the American dream and the idea that if one works hard enough that person will succeed. However, despite his hard work, the executive has had a number of recent business failures, including losing a substantial sum of money in the stock market. To make matters worse, his children need braces. To live up to expectations, become a success, and provide for his family, the executive had to steal the money from his business.

Passage 3

Regular exercise protects people against getting sick during the cold and flu season. According to a recent study of 1,000 adult volunteers over a three-month period, those who exercised at least five times a week had 43 percent fewer days of illness than those who exercised less than one day a week.

Sample Responses

Passage 1

CONCLUSION: *Eating oranges helps alleviate depression.*

REASON: *9 of 13 patients who ate oranges experienced improvement with their depression.*

Can anything else account for the change besides eating oranges? Yes; the researcher fails to rule out many obvious alternative explanations. For example, the patients might have *expected* to get better, and these *expectancies* might have led to feeling better. Also, they knew the purpose of eating oranges, and a rival cause is that they *tried to please* the researchers by reporting that they felt better. We can also hypothesize that external events during the three-week treatment period caused the change. Perhaps during the three weeks of treatment, for example, the weather was especially good, and these people spent much more time exercising outside than usual, which could also help alleviate depression. Another possibility is that these people were suffering from a form of depression from which they could naturally expect to recover in a short period of time. Can you locate other rival causes?

Passage 2

CONCLUSION: *The executive stole money from his company to compete with his family members, to show that he is not a failure, and to provide for his family.*

REASON: *The executive was probably concerned with all of the above elements.*

It is possible that all of the above factors were important in causing the corporate executive to steal from his company. But many other people in society have the same pressures put upon them, and they do not resort to illegal means to obtain money. Are there other possible causes for such behavior? As in the case of the Fort Hood massacre, there may be many other plausible explanations. For example, we would want to know more about his childhood and more about recent events in his life. Has the corporate executive had any recent disagreements with his boss? Had he been using drugs? Had he had any recent highly stressful experiences? Did he have a history of stealing? After the fact, we can always find childhood experiences that make sense as causes of adult behavior. Before we draw causal conclusions, however, we must seek more evidence to prove that one set of events caused the other than the mere fact that one set of events preceded the other set. We must also be wary not to fall victims to the fundamental attribution error and be certain to consider external causal factors, as well as internal ones.

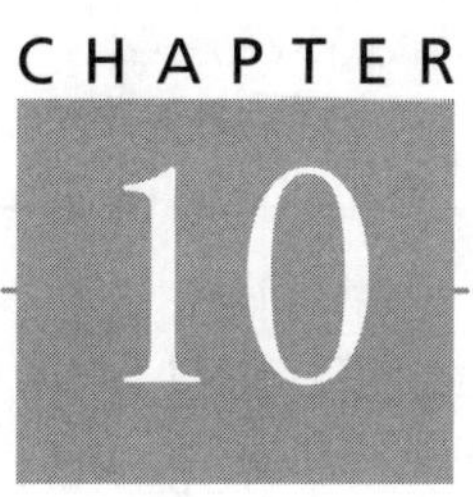

Are the Statistics Deceptive?

How much should you be persuaded by the following passage?

> News bulletin: The economy is greatly improving. Last month alone our unemployment rate decreased by 1 percent.

You should not be very impressed by the above reasoning. The argument *deceives us with statistics!*

One of the most frequent kinds of evidence that authors present is "statistics." You have probably often heard people use the following phrase to help support their argument: "I have statistics to prove it." We use statistics (often inappropriately) to reveal increases or decreases in war casualties, to alert the public to changing disease rates, to measure the sales of a new product, to judge the moneymaking capabilities of certain stocks, to determine the likelihood of the next card being the ace, to measure graduation rates for different colleges, to record the frequency of different groups having sex, and to provide input for many other issues.

Statistics are evidence expressed as numbers. Such evidence can seem quite impressive because numbers make evidence appear to be very scientific and precise, as though it represents "the facts." *Statistics, however, can, and often do, lie!* They do not necessarily prove what they appear to prove.

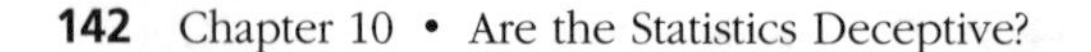

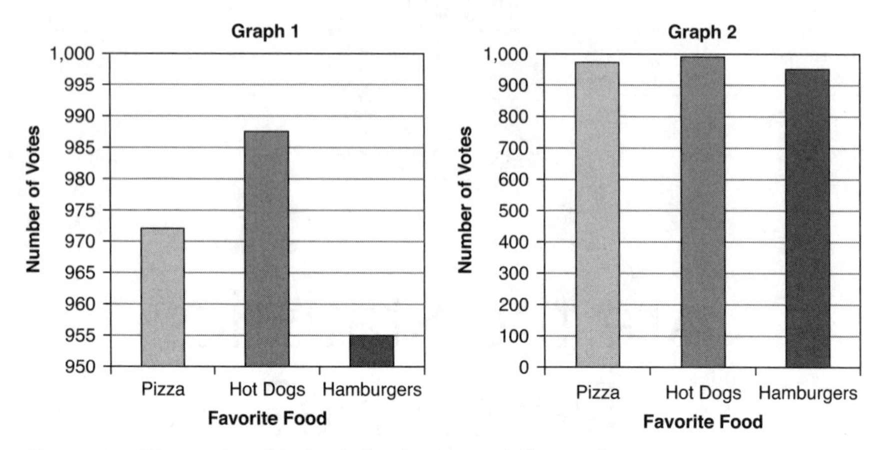

Alternative Ways to Provide Statistics that Potentially Deceive

***Attention:** Statistics can and often lie. They do not necessarily prove what they appear to prove.*

As a critical thinker, you should strive to detect erroneous statistical reasoning. In a few short paragraphs, we cannot show you all the different ways that people can "lie with statistics." However, this chapter will provide some general strategies that you can use to detect such deception. Also, it will alert you to flaws in statistical reasoning by illustrating a number of the most common ways that authors misuse statistical evidence.

Critical Question: ***Are the statistics deceptive?***

UNKNOWABLE AND BIASED STATISTICS

> Recent headline: 40 PERCENT OF COLLEGE STUDENTS SUFFER FROM DEPRESSION!

Should you be unduly alarmed that you're feeling sad? How do you know that you can trust that statistic?

Any statistic requires that some events somewhere have been *defined* and *accurately identified*, which are often very difficult tasks. Thus, the first strategy for locating deceptive statistics is to try to find out as much as you can about how the statistics were obtained. Can we know precisely the number of people in the United States who cheat on their taxes, have premarital sex, talk on their cell phones while driving, or use illegal drugs? If you imagined the details of doing such counts, we suspect your answer is "Not likely." Why? Because there are a variety of obstacles to getting accurate statistics for certain purposes, including ambiguity of key terms, difficulties in identifying relevant persons or events, people's unwillingness to provide truthful information, people's failure to report events, and physical barriers to observing events.

Consequently, statistics are often in the form of educated guesses. Such estimates can be useful; they can also be deceiving. Always ask, "How did the author arrive at the estimate?" The more detail you get, the better.

One common use of unknowable statistics is to impress or alarm others with large numbers, often presenting them with a suspicious precision. For example, large numbers may be used to try to alert the public to the increasing incidence of physical or mental disorders, such as cancer, eating disorders, or childhood autism. We want to be most impressed by these numbers if we know how carefully they were determined. For example, the issue of unknowable numbers has been a major factor in the efforts to establish accurate counts of the rate of depression in college students, with research-reported rates varying from 10 percent to 40 percent. So, maybe it's premature to be overly alarmed by the study mentioned at the beginning of this section. *Remember:* Before reacting to such statistics, we need to ask how they were determined.

CONFUSING AVERAGES

Examine the following statements:

1. One way to make money fast is to become a professional football player. An **average** NFL football player made $1.8 million in 2010.
2. Making the grade in college classes is requiring less work for students; according to a recent survey, college students are studying an **average** of 12.8 hours per week, about half of the hours studied 20 years ago.

Both examples use the word "average." But there are three different ways to determine an average, and in most cases, each will give you a different value.

One way is to add all the values and divide this total by the number of values used. The result is the *mean.* A second way is to list all the values from highest to lowest, then find the one in the middle. This middle value is the *median.* Half of the values will be above the *median*; half will be below it. A third way is to list all the values and then count each different value or each range of values. The value that appears most frequently is called the *mode*, the third kind of average.

It makes a big difference whether a writer is talking about the mean, median, or mode.

EXHIBIT 10-1 Types of Averages

✓ Mean	Determined by adding all the values and dividing by the total number of values
✓ Median	Determined by listing all the numbers from highest to lowest and finding the one in the middle
✓ Mode	Determined by counting the frequency of different values and then finding the value that appears most frequently

What average makes the most sense in the first example? Consider the salaries of the stars versus those of the average players in professional sports. The biggest stars, such as the star quarterback, will make much higher salaries than most other players on the team. In fact, the highest paid football players for the year 2010 made more than $15 million—well above the average. Such high salaries will increase the mean dramatically, but will have no major effect on the median or mode. For example, the mean salary for NFL players in 2010 was $1.8 million, but the median salary was "only" $770,000. Thus, in most professional sports, the mean salaries will be much higher than the median or modal salaries. Consequently, if one wished to make the salaries seem extremely high, one would choose the mean as the indicator of the average.

Now, let's look carefully at the second example. If the average presented is either the mode or the median, we may be overestimating the average amount of study time. Some students likely put in a very high number of study hours, such as 30 or 40 hours per week, thus raising the value of the mean but not affecting the value of the mode or median. The modal study-hour value could be significantly lower or higher than the median, depending on what number of study hours is most frequent for students.

When you see "average" values, always ask, "Does it matter whether it is the mean, the median, or the mode?" To answer this question, consider how using the various meanings of average might change the significance of the information.

Not only is it important to determine whether an average is a mean, median, or mode, but it is also often important to determine the gap between the smallest and largest values—the *range*—and how frequently each of the values occurs—the *distribution*.

Let's consider an example in which knowing the range and distribution would be important.

> Doctor speaking to 20-year-old patient: The prognosis for your cancer is very poor. The median length of survival is 10 months. You should spend the next few months of your life doing those things that you have always wanted to do.

How dire should the patient view his future after receiving such a diagnosis? First, all we know for sure is that half of the people with this diagnosis die within 10 months, and half live longer than 10 months. But we don't know the range and distribution of how much longer the surviving half lives! The range and distribution of people who live more than 10 months could reveal that some or many people live well beyond 10 more months. Some, or even many, may live past 80! Knowing the complete survival distribution could change how this cancer victim views his future.

In general, a patient should consider whether different hospitals in the country have different ranges and distributions of survival for his disorder.

If so, he should consider choosing treatment at the hospital with the most favorable distribution.

A general benefit of keeping the range and distribution in mind when encountering averages is that doing so should remind you that most people or events will not match the exact average value and that outcomes quite discrepant from the average are to be expected. For example, many interventions to improve our health will show an **average gain** in some health measure even though many people in the study may show little or no gain, and some will even show a loss.

CONCLUDING ONE THING, PROVING ANOTHER

Communicators often deceive us when they use statistics that prove one thing but then claim to have proved something quite different. The statistics don't prove what they seem to! We suggest two strategies for locating such deception.

One strategy is to *blind yourself to the communicator's statistics* and ask yourself, "What statistical evidence would be helpful in proving her conclusion?" Then, compare the "needed" statistics to the statistics given. If the two do not match, you may have located a statistical deception. The following example provides you with an opportunity to apply that strategy.

> A new weight-loss drug, Fatsaway, is effective in helping obese people lose weight. In a clinical trial, only 6 out of 100 people on Fatsaway reported any side effects with taking the drug. The company manufacturing the drug argues, "With 94 percent of people having positive results with Fatsaway, it is safe to say our pill is one of the most effective weight-loss pills in the market."

How should the company manufacturing the drug have proven its conclusion that Fatsaway is 94 percent effective as a weight-loss pill? Shouldn't it have performed a study of how many people lost weight with the pill, and how much weight these people lost? Instead, the company reported statistics regarding the frequency of side effects and has assumed that if the pill did not produce side effects, then the pill was effective in helping people lose weight. The company proves one thing (a relatively small number of people report side effects with Fatsaway) and concludes another (Fatsaway is effective at helping people lose weight). An important lesson to learn from this example is to *pay close attention to both the wording of the statistics and the wording of the conclusion* to see whether both are referring to the same thing. When they are not, the author or speaker may be lying with statistics.

Knowing just what statistical evidence should be provided to support a conclusion is difficult. Thus, another strategy is to examine the author's statistics *very closely* while *blinding yourself to the conclusion*; then ask yourself, "What is the appropriate conclusion to be drawn from those statistics?" Then, compare your conclusion with the author's. Try that strategy with the following example.

> Almost half of all Americans cheat on their significant others. A researcher recently interviewed people at a shopping mall. Of the 75 people responding to the survey, 36 admitted to having friends who had admitted cheating on someone they were seeing.

Did you come up with the following conclusion? Almost half of the people *in one given location* admit to *having friends* who report having cheated, *at least once*, on someone with whom they were dating or were otherwise involved. Do you see the difference between what the statistics proved and what the author concluded? If so, you have discovered how this author has lied with statistics.

DECEIVING BY OMITTING INFORMATION

Statistics often deceive us because they are incomplete. Thus, a further helpful strategy for locating flaws in statistical reasoning is to ask, "*What further information do you need before you can judge the impact of the statistics?*" Let's look at the following examples to illustrate the usefulness of this question.

1. Large businesses are destroying the small town feel of our downtown area. Just last year, the number of large businesses in the city has increased by 75 percent.
2. Despite common fears, skydiving is much safer than other activities such as driving a car. In one particular month, in Los Angeles, 176 people died in car accidents while only 3 died in skydiving accidents.
3. AIDS prevention programs need major funding increases. In 2009, 54,000 people were afflicted with AIDS.

In the first example, 75 percent seems quite impressive. But something is missing: The *absolute numbers* on which this percentage is based. Wouldn't we be less alarmed if we knew that this increase was from 4 businesses to 7, rather than from 12 to 21? In our second example, we have the numbers, but we don't have the *percentages*. Wouldn't we need to know what these numbers mean in terms of percentages of people involved in both activities? After all, there are fewer total skydivers than there are people traveling in cars.

The third example illustrates a common occurrence in our society, an attempt to arouse the public's attention to a societal problem by spotlighting the number of people afflicted nationally. Although clearly an urgent problem, when we divide 54,000 by the approximate population of the United States, 300 million, we get a value of about 0.02 percent.

When you encounter impressive-sounding numbers or percentages, beware! You may need to get other information to decide just how impressive the numbers are. When only *absolute numbers* are presented, ask whether *percentages* might help you make a better judgment; when only *percentages* are presented, ask whether *absolute numbers* would enrich their meaning.

Another important kind of potential missing information is *relevant comparisons*. It is often useful to ask the question, "As compared to . . .?"

Each of the following statements illustrates statistics that can benefit from asking for comparisons:

- Medusa hair spray, now 50 percent better.
- SUVs are dangerous and should not be allowed on the road. In 2006, there were 4,650 occupant deaths in SUV accidents. Certainly, something needs to be done.
- Movie budgets are outrageous nowadays. Just look at *Harry Potter and the Goblet of Fire*; the budget for that movie is $308,000,000!
- More evidence that our culture is dumbing down is provided by the fact that a recent *New York Times* article reported that fewer than half of teenagers interviewed knew when the Civil War was fought.

With reference to the first statement, don't you need to ask, "50 percent better than what?" Other ineffective hair sprays? Previous Medusa brand hair spray? As for the second statement, wouldn't you want to know how many of those deaths would have been prevented if an SUV were not involved, how many other motor vehicle fatalities not involving an SUV were there, how many SUVs were on the road compared to the number of deaths they were involved in, and how many miles SUVs travel compared to how many deaths occur in SUVs? With reference to the third statement, how does the budget of one particular movie relate to the budget of other movies, and is this one case highly unusual, or is it typical of the movie industry? As for knowledge of Civil War dates, how do these findings compare to results from a similar survey completed 20 years ago?

When you encounter statistics, be sure to ask, "What relevant information is missing?"

RISK STATISTICS AND OMITTED INFORMATION

> Eating too much high fat meat every day increases the likelihood of bowel cancer by 25 percent.
>
> Results from the new cancer drug were disappointing, showing an absolute reduction in breast cancer of only 0.5 percent.

A common use of statistics in arguments—especially arguments about health risks—is the reporting of risk reduction as a result of some intervention. Such reports can be deceptive. The same amount of risk reduction can be reported in many forms, such as in *relative versus absolute terms*, and these differences can greatly affect our perceptions of the actual amount of risk reduction.

Imagine a 65-year-old woman who just had a stroke and is discussing treatment options with her doctor. The doctor quotes statistics about three treatment options:

(1) Treatment X will *reduce the likelihood* of a future stroke by 33 percent,
(2) Treatment Y will *reduce the absolute risk* by 3 percent, from 6 percent to 3 percent, and
(3) With treatment Z, 94 percent of women are free of a second stroke for 10 years, compared to 91 percent of those who go untreated.

Which treatment should she choose? Our guess is that you will select the first. But all of these options refer to the same-size treatment effect. They just express the risk in different ways. The first (the 33 percent) is the *relative risk reduction*. If a treatment reduces the risk of heart attack from 9 in 100 to 6 in 100, the risk is reduced by one-third, or 33 percent, that is, 9 minus 6 divided by 9, or the risk without treatment minus the risk with treatment divided by the risk without treatment. But the *absolute* change, from 9 to 6 percent, is only a 3 percent reduction, and the improvement of a good outcome from 91 to 94 is also only 3 percent. The point is that expressing risk reductions in relative, rather than absolute, terms can make treatment effects seem larger than they really are, and individuals are more likely to embrace a treatment when benefits are expressed in relative rather than absolute terms. As you might expect, drug companies usually use relative risk in their ads, and media reports also tend to focus on relative risk.

Do you see how you might respond differently to our two risk examples at the beginning of this section knowing that the absolute increase in bowel cancer rate was from 4 percent to 5 percent and the decrease in absolute cancer rate was from 1 percent to 0.5 percent? When you encounter arguments using such statistics, always try to determine just how risk deductions were determined and how the results might be different and less or more impressive if expressed in absolute terms.

USING STATISTICS IN YOUR WRITING

We hope that you incorporate statistics into your writing. When used appropriately, they are a valuable tool. They help us describe and understand trends and patterns. They help us to predict. Statistics can strengthen our arguments. Even so, this chapter has illuminated some of the very serious risks of incorporating statistics into an argument. To the untrained reader, statistics look like authoritative facts, but you know how easily the facts can be manipulated. As a writer concerned with critical thinking, you are faced with an important balancing act. You must attempt to avoid deceptive techniques, but also present often-complicated statistics in a clear and understandable way.

Have you noticed that the statistics that seem easiest to understand are often the poorest quality? Think about the reader polls in *Marie Claire*, *USA Today*, and *New York Times Magazine* or consumer surveys on Amazon or Priceline. These statistics are certainly easy to read. For instance, *Time* magazine reported its Readers' Choice for Person of the Year in 2010: "Julian Assange raked in 382,020 votes, giving him an easy first place. He was 148,383 votes over the silver medalist, Recep Tayyip Erdogan, prime minister of Turkey." As of December 2010, 101 out of 152 reviewers on Amazon thought that *Glee: The Complete First Season* was a five-star product. These statistics seem cut and dried, right? You know better now. You know now that these facts are missing information. We do not know how many times a person could vote for person of the year. We know that neither sample was random—the voting was Web-based, so it probably excluded many older, less technological savvy readers in favor of younger or more computer-adept readers.

To make careful arguments with statistics, you may have to take some time away from your argument to explain how the statistics were produced, the implications of the statistics, and the limitations of them. Doing so will improve your credibility with your readers. You are showing them that you are not trying to sneak something by them. You are also encouraging them to be strong-sensed critical thinkers and draw their own conclusions about the quality of the statistics. You may decide to include these explanations in the text of your argument, or you could chose to include them in a footnote, endnote, or in an appendix. This decision will likely be based on the habit of your field and formality of the writing.

Clues for Assessing Statistics

1. Try to find out as much as you can about how the statistics were obtained. Ask, "*How does the author or speaker know?*" Be especially vigilant when the communicator tries to impress or alarm you with large numbers.
2. Be curious about the type of average being described; analyze whether knowing the range and distribution of events would add a helpful perspective to the statistic.
3. Be alert to users of statistics concluding one thing, but proving another.
4. Blind yourself to the writer's or speaker's statistics and compare the needed statistical evidence with the statistics actually provided.
5. Form your own conclusion from the statistics. If it doesn't match the author's or speaker's conclusion, then something is probably wrong.
6. Determine what information is missing. Be especially alert for misleading numbers and percentages and for missing comparisons.

PRACTICE EXERCISES

? *Critical Question:* ***Are the statistics deceptive?***

For each of the practice passages, identify inadequacies in the evidence.

Passage 1

Campaigns for national office are getting out of hand. Money is playing a central role in more and more elections. The average winner in a senate race now spends over $8 million on his or her campaign, while typical presidential candidates spend more than $300 million. It is time for some serious changes, because we cannot simply allow politicians to buy their seats through large expenditures on advertisements.

Passage 2

The home is becoming a more dangerous place to spend time. The number of home-related injuries is on the rise. In 2000, approximately 2,300 children aged 14 and under died from accidents in the home. Also, 4.7 million people are bitten by dogs each year. To make matters worse, even television, a relatively safe household appliance, is becoming dangerous. In fact, 42,000 people are injured by televisions and television stands each year. With so many accidents in the home, perhaps people need to start spending more time outdoors.

Passage 3

Aggressive counseling reduces troops' mental problems. A recent study of 10,000 soldiers during a major battle surge conducted by the army revealed that more aggressive counseling methods decreased the risk of suicide attempts by soldiers by more than 50 percent.

Sample Responses

Passage 1

CONCLUSION: *A change in campaigning for national office is necessary.*

REASON: *Politicians are spending too much on campaigns. The average senator spent more than $8 million on his or her campaign. Presidential candidates spend more than $300 million on their campaigns.*

Are campaigns costing too much money? The words *average* and *typical* should alert us to a potential deception. We need to know the kind of average used for these statistics. Was it the mean, median, or the mode? For example, using the mean in the senate race data could potentially lead to a figure that is skewed because of certain, particularly close, senate races where candidates spent large sums of money. However, because many senators are basically guaranteed reelection, these races probably involve less spending. We know that only a few senate race elections are unusually close. Therefore, most probably do not spend as much as was reported, if the mean was used to present the average. In other words, the median or the mode would probably show a lower value. Also, knowing the distribution and range would give you a better idea of how much you would want to be concerned about campaign spending practices.

Additionally, important comparison figures are missing. How does campaign spending compare to similar spending in the past? What about for other offices? It is possible that campaign spending has actually gone down in recent years.

Passage 2

CONCLUSION: *It is becoming increasingly dangerous to spend time in one's home.*

REASONS: *Household-related injuries are on the rise.*

SUPPORT: *In one year, 2,300 children died in household accidents.*
4.7 million people are bitten by dogs every year.
42,000 people are injured by televisions each year.

To evaluate the argument, we need to first determine what the most appropriate evidence is to answer the question, "Are households more unsafe than they used to be?" In our opinion, the best statistic to use to answer the preceding question is a comparison of the current rate of serious household accidents per year with the rate in past years.. Also relevant is the number of injuries per hour spent in the house versus the same statistic for past years. It is possible that more household injuries occur because people are spending more time in their houses than they used to spend. If they are inside the house more, it is only logical that the number of injuries occurring in the house would also rise.

The evidence presented in the argument is questionable for a number of other reasons. First, no number is given at all regarding the total number of household injuries. We know the author says they are on the rise, but no evidence is provided demonstrating a rise. Second, no details are given regarding the deaths of children in household accidents. How does this statistic compare to children's deaths in the home in the past? What types of accidents are causing these children's deaths? Third, the number of dog bites is deceptive. We do not know whether these dog bites occur in the home. More importantly, the number of dog bites does not seem to move us toward the conclusion that being at home is unsafe. Fourth, the statistic regarding televisions is questionable. Where does the author get the impressive sounding statistic? Also, how serious are most of these injuries?

What Significant Information Is Omitted?

How compelling is the following advertisement?

> Try HappyTyme, the number one doctor-prescribed treatment for depression.

The purpose of the advertisement is, of course, to persuade you to buy more of the designated product. Even before your critical-thinking skills developed to their current level, you knew that such advertisements tell less than the whole truth. For example, if the HappyTyme Company gives a bigger discount to psychiatrists than do other pharmaceutical companies, provides psychiatrists with greater numbers of free samples, or provides cruises for psychiatrists who use their product, you are unlikely to see this information included in the advertisement. You will not see that information, but it is quite relevant to your decision about what to take for your depression.

While critical thinkers are seeking the strength of autonomy, they cannot do so if they are making decisions on the basis of highly limited information. Almost any conclusion or product has some positive characteristics. Those who have an interest in telling us only the information they want us to know will tell us all of these positive characteristics in great and vivid detail. But they will hide the negative aspects of their conclusions. Thus, actual autonomy requires our persistent search for what is being hidden, either accidentally or on purpose.

By asking questions learned in previous chapters, such as those concerning ambiguity, assumptions, and evidence, you will detect much important missing information. This chapter tries to sensitize you even more to the importance of *what is not said* and to serve as an important reminder that we react to an incomplete picture of an argument when we evaluate only the *explicit* parts. We thus devote this chapter to an extremely important additional question you must ask to judge the quality of reasoning: What significant information is omitted?

*Critical Question: **What significant information is omitted?***

THE BENEFITS OF DETECTING OMITTED INFORMATION

You should remember that almost any information that you encounter has a purpose. In other words, its organization was selected and presented by someone who hoped that it would affect your thinking in some way. Hence, your task is to decide whether you wish to be an instrument of the chosen purpose. Often that purpose is to persuade you.

Advertisers, teachers, politicians, authors, speakers, researchers, bloggers, and parents all organize information to shape your decisions. Thus, those trying to persuade you will almost always try to present their position in the strongest possible light. So, when you find what you believe to be persuasive reasons—those gold nuggets for which you are prospecting—it's wise to hesitate and to think about what the author may *not* have told you, something that your critical questioning has not yet revealed.

By *significant omitted information*, we mean information that would affect whether you should be influenced by a speaker's or writer's arguments—information that *shapes the reasoning*! Interspersed throughout the chapter will be examples of reasoning that are not very convincing, not because of what is said but because of what is omitted. Study the examples carefully and notice how in each case the failure to look for omitted information would have resulted in your making a premature and potentially erroneous judgment.

***Attention:** Significant omitted information is information that shapes the reasoning.*

THE CERTAINTY OF INCOMPLETE REASONING

Incomplete reasoning is inevitable for several reasons. First, there is the limitation imposed by time and space. Arguments are incomplete because communicators do not have forever to organize them, nor do they have unlimited space or time in which to present their reasons.

Second, most of us have a very limited attention span; we get bored when messages are too long. Thus, communicators often feel a need to get their message across quickly. Advertisements and editorials reflect both these factors. For example, editorials are limited to a specific number of words, and the argument must both be interesting and make the author's point. Editorial writers, therefore, engage in many annoying omissions. Television commentators are notorious for making highly complicated issues sound as if they are simple. They have very little time to provide the degree of accurate information that you will need to form a reasonable conclusion.

A third reason for the inevitability of missing information is that the knowledge possessed by the person making the argument will always be incomplete. A fourth reason why information may be omitted is because of an outright attempt to deceive. Advertisers *know* they are omitting key bits of information. If they were to describe all the chemicals or cheap component parts that go into their products, you would be less likely to buy those products. Experts in every field consciously omit information when open disclosure would weaken the persuasive effect of their advice. Such omissions are particularly tempting if those trying to advise you see you as a "sponge."

A final important reason why omitted information is so prevalent is that the values, beliefs, and attitudes of those trying to advise or persuade you are frequently different from yours. You can expect, therefore, that their reasoning will be guided by different assumptions from those you would have brought to the same question. Critical thinkers value curiosity and reasonableness; those working to persuade you often want to extinguish your curiosity and to encourage you to rely on unreasonable emotional responses to shape your choices.

A particular perspective is like a pair of blinders on a horse. The blinders improve the tendency of the horse to focus on what is directly in front of it. Yet, an individual's perspective, like blinders on a horse, prevents that person from noting certain information that would be important to those who reason from a different frame of reference. Actor Matt Damon's character shows an understanding of this important point in *The Bourne Ultimatum*: "It's funny how different things look, depending on where you sit." Unless

EXHIBIT 11-1 Reasons for Incomplete Reasoning

- ✓ Time and space imposes limitations on arguments.
- ✓ Arguments must be given quickly due to limited attention spans.
- ✓ The arguer will always have incomplete knowledge.
- ✓ Arguments often attempt to deceive.
- ✓ The arguer often will have different values, belief, and attitudes from yours.

your perspective is identical to that of the person trying to persuade you, important omissions of information are to be expected.

QUESTIONS THAT IDENTIFY OMITTED INFORMATION

How do you identify omitted information? First you have to remind yourself that regardless of how attractive the reasons supporting a particular decision or opinion may initially seem, you need to take another look in search of omitted information.

How do you search, and what can you expect to find? You ask questions to help decide what additional information you need, and then ask questions designed to reveal that information.

You can use many kinds of questions to identify relevant omitted information. Some questions you have already learned to ask will highlight such information. In addition, to help you determine omitted information that might get overlooked by other critical questions, we provide you with a list of some important kinds of omitted information and some examples of questions to help detect them.

Being aware of these specific types should help you a lot in locating relevant omitted information. Because so many kinds of important omitted information exist, however, you should always ask yourself the general question, "Has the speaker or writer left out any other information that I need to know before I judge the reasoning quality?" Let's examine a few arguments that have omitted some of the types of information just listed and watch how each omission might cause us to form a faulty conclusion. Only by asking that omitted information be supplied in each case could you avoid this danger. Initially, let's look at an advertising claim.

> Zitout brand facial cleanser removes 95 percent of deep-down dirt and oil, helping to fight unsightly blemishes.

Should we all run out and buy Zitout facial cleanser? Wait just a minute! Among many omissions, the advertisement fails to include any of the following information: (a) percentage of deep-down dirt and oil other facial cleansers remove; maybe they remove 99 percent of dirt and oil; (b) amount of dirt and oil removed by washing with soap alone; it might be possible that faces can be cleaned adequately with normal soap; (c) potential negative consequences of using this specific product; it is possible that some of the ingredients might cause excessive dryness or pose cancer risks; (d) other sources of blemishes; perhaps dirt and oil are not the highest concerns when washing one's face; (e) amount of dirt and oil necessary to cause blemishes; maybe 5 percent will still cause a significant number of blemishes; and (f) other advantages or disadvantages of the facial cleanser, such as smell, price, and length of effective action. The advertiser has omitted much significant data that you would need if you were to buy wisely.

Clues for Finding Common Kinds of Significant Information

1. Common counterarguments
   a. What reasons would someone who disagrees offer?
   b. Are there research studies that contradict the studies presented?
   c. Are there missing examples, testimonials, and opinions from well-respected authorities, or analogies that support the other side of the argument?
2. Missing definitions
   a. How would the arguments differ if key terms were defined in other ways?
3. Missing value preferences or perspectives
   a. Would different values create a different approach to this issue?
   b. What arguments would flow from values different from those of the speaker or writer?
4. Origins of "facts" referred to in the argument
   a. What is the source for the "facts"?
   b. Are the factual claims supported by competent research or by reliable sources?
5. Details of procedures used for gathering facts
   a. How many people completed the questionnaire?
   b. How are the survey questions worded?
   c. Did respondents have ample opportunity to provide answers different from those reported by the person using the responses?
6. Alternative techniques for gathering or organizing the evidence
   a. How might the results from an interview study differ from written questionnaire results?
   b. Would a laboratory experiment have created more reliable and informative results?
7. Missing or incomplete figures, graphs, tables, or data
   a. Would the data look different if they included evidence from earlier or later years?
   b. Has the author "stretched" the figure to make the differences look larger?
8. Omitted effects, both positive and negative and both short and long term, of what is advocated and what is opposed
   a. Has the argument left out important positive or negative consequences of a proposed action? What are the costs? What are the benefits?
   b. Do we need to know the impact of the action on any of the following areas: political, social, economic, biological, spiritual, health, or environmental?
9. Omission of prediction failures, or misses, when arguing for special prediction skills.
   a. When "psychics" or "intuitionists" promote their special abilities, we need to ask how often their predictions have proven to be untrue.
   b. We need to know the frequency of prediction failures, as well of successes, of economists, financial advisers, sports gamblers, and political pundits before concluding that they have special expertise.

Do you see how advertising phrases like "four out of five doctors agree," "all natural," "fat free," "low in carbs," "good for your heart," "number 1 leading brand," "ADA approved," and "no added preservatives" may all be accurate but misleading because of omitted information?

THE IMPORTANCE OF THE NEGATIVE VIEW

There is one type of omitted information that is so important to identify and so often overlooked that we want to specifically highlight it for you: the *potential negative effects* of actions being advocated, such as the use of a new medication, the building of a large new school, or a proposed tax cut. We stress the negative effects here because usually proposals for such action occur in the context of backers' heralding their benefits, such as greater reduction of a certain medical problem, better appearance, more leisure, more educational opportunities, increased length of life, and more and/or improved commodities. However, because most actions have such widespread positive *and negative* impacts, we need to ask:

- Which segments of society do not benefit from a proposed action? Who loses? What do the losers have to say about it?
- How does the proposed action affect the distribution of power?
- What are the action's effects on our health?
- How does the action influence our relationships with one another? With the natural environment?

For each of these questions, we always have to ask, "What are the potential *long-term negative effects* of the action?"

***Attention:* Remember to ask, "What are the potential long-term negative effects of the action?" when considering omitted information.**

To illustrate the usefulness of asking these questions, let's reflect upon the following question: What are some possible negative effects of building a large new school? Did you think of the following?

- Destruction of the environment. For example, would building a new school involve the removal of a wooded area? How would the local wildlife be affected by the potential loss of a habitat?
- *Shifts in quality of education provided.* What if the new school attracts skilled teachers or gifted students away from other schools? What if the new school absorbed a significant amount of the funds available to schools, depriving other schools of the same funds?
- *Effects of property values.* If the school does not do well in comparison with national standards, how will this affect the property values of the houses in the surrounding community?
- *Increased tax burden.* How would the new school be funded? If the new school is a public school, the opening of the new school could result in an increase in property taxes for the local community to help support the new school.

Questions such as these can give us pause for thought before jumping on the bandwagon of a proposed action.

OMITTED INFORMATION THAT REMAINS MISSING

Just because you are able to request important missing information does not guarantee a satisfactory response. It is quite possible that your probing questions cannot be answered. Do not despair! You did your part. You requested information that you needed to make up your mind; you must now decide whether it is possible to arrive at a conclusion without the missing information. We warned you earlier that reasoning is always incomplete. Therefore, to claim automatically that you cannot make a decision as long as information is missing would prevent you from ever forming any opinions.

MISSING INFORMATION IN YOUR OWN ARGUMENTS

Omitting information is unavoidable. We do not expect you to take on every question we listed earlier in the chapter. Instead, in your writing, we ask you to make a judgment call. You must decide what omitted information is most important. A piece of omitted information is important when it has the ability to strongly influence your readers' position on your argument. You must ask yourself, "If my readers knew that information, how might that influence their reactions to my argument?" The more influence you think it may have, the more important it is that you avoid omitting the information from your writing.

Although we cannot make your judgment call, we do have a few suggestions. They resemble some of our earlier techniques. Let's imagine that you are trying to determine whether you have omitted information you should have included, such as a counterargument or a research study that contradicts your evidence. One way of making such a determination is to return to your original research. What are the crucial points they are debating? For instance, if you were writing about who should have won the Academy Award for best picture in 2010, you could immerse yourself in the debate among top reviewers about their favorites and why. You may realize that you had neglected to mention *The Social Network*, the fictionalized drama about the founding of Facebook, and that a number of reviewers considered it a top contender for the award. Even if you disagreed with these conclusions, you learned that the reviewers' positions were influential. You also learned that you need not share with your readers the merits of Angelina Jolie and Johnny Depp's movie *The Tourist*. Based on poor overall reviews, you determined that any promotion of this film for best picture was probably trivial.

Our next suggestion should also sound familiar. Take advantage of the people in your life, particularly those who hold different value preferences and beliefs about the world. Ask them what information they would need to know to accept your argument. These conversations may direct you to significant information that you have omitted. In a similar vein, you can explore this question alone through some creative thinking. Imagine a diverse group of your potential readers and try to put yourself in their shoes. For instance, think of a reader with a different political persuasion or cultural identity, or just a different set of personal priorities. From that perspective, imagine what information that person would like to access before weighing your argument. Can they find it in your writing?

USING THIS CRITICAL QUESTION

Once you have thought about the existence of missing information in an argument, what should you do? The first logical reaction is to seek the information. But usually you will encounter resistance. Your options as a critical thinker are to voice your displeasure with the argument in light of the missing information, keep searching for the information that you require, or cautiously agree with the reasoning on the grounds that this argument is better than its competitors.

PRACTICE EXERCISES

Critical Question: ***What significant information is omitted?***

In each of the following examples, there is important missing information. Make a list of questions you would ask the person who wrote each passage. Explain in each case why the information you are seeking is important to you as you try to decide the worth of the reasoning.

Passage 1

A recent research study suggests that abstaining from alcohol tends to shorten life expectancy; even more striking is the fact that teetotalers' mortality rates are greater than those of heavy drinkers. Moderate drinking, defined as one to three drinks per day, is associated with the lowest mortality rates. Over a 20-year period, mortality rates were highest for those who were not current drinkers, regardless of whether they used to be alcoholics, second highest for heavy drinkers and lowest for moderate drinkers. The sample included 1,824 participants, ranging from 55 to 65 years of age at the beginning of the 20-year study. The death rates were: teetotalers, 69 percent; heavy drinkers, 60 percent; and moderate drinkers, 41 percent. Researchers suggested that an important reason for heavy drinkers living longer than those who don't drink is the social lubricating effect of social interactions.

Passage 2

Cloning technology can lead to many positive breakthroughs in the medical field. If we were to adequately develop cloning technology, there would no longer be a need for people to die because of a lack of organ donors. With cloning, researchers could artificially develop new organs for people in need of transplants. Plus, because these organs would be cloned from the person's own tissues, there would be no chance of his or her body rejecting the transplanted organ. The cloned organs can be made in bodies that lack a head, and thus would not involve a "death" in order to save a life. Another advantage of cloning is that it can help fight disease. Certain proteins produced by clones can be used to fight diseases such as diabetes, Parkinson's disease, and cystic fibrosis.

Passage 3

America is the policeman of the world. It is our job to go into countries that need our help and to watch over them. One effective way to limit the interactions we need to have with other countries is to encourage the development of democracy and free markets in these countries. After all, the modern Western democracies have not fought wars against one another, and they are all democratic with a free market structure. Furthermore, look at the easy transition Germany had when it was reunited. Democracy was installed and the formerly split West and East Germany came along just fine. In fact, the German economy did really well with the transition also. Germany currently has the third largest GDP of any country in the world, all because of democracy and capitalism.

Sample Responses

Passage 1

CONCLUSION: *Heavy drinkers live longer than those who don't drink, and moderate drinkers live longest of all.*

REASON: *A recent research study found this ranking of longevity.*

Omitted information analysis. In what other ways, such as socioeconomic class and life stressors, do these three groups differ from each other that might cause the difference in death rate? What are the possible negative effects of moderate and heavy drinking? Are there possibly effects on memory, satisfaction in marriage, and job performance? Have these results been found in other studies? How were participants selected? For example, do volunteers for such studies differ from a random sample, thus limiting the generalization? How was drinking frequency measured? Was it accurate?

Passage 2

CONCLUSION: *Cloning can provide positive medical benefits.*

REASONS: 1. *Clones can be used for human transplants.*

2. *Clones can be used to help combat certain diseases.*

First, this reasoning urges us to pursue a new technology—human cloning—and cites only its advantages. The writer omits possible disadvantages. We need to consider both advantages and disadvantages. What serious side effects might result from using cloned organs? Are cloned organs as stable as regular organs? What positive and negative effects might cloning technology have on human decision making? Would people be less likely to take care of their bodies and their organs if they knew that new organs could be grown to replace their current ones? Would the availability of the technology lead people to misuse cloning to produce complete human clones for an insidious purpose? Would people clone themselves, helping add to the burden already placed on Earth by the current population? The advantages of the procedure may well outweigh the disadvantages, but we need to be aware of both in judging the merits of the conclusion.

Furthermore, let's look at the missing information regarding the research. Did you notice that no research has been cited? In fact, the argument fails to tell us that no tests on human cloning have occurred in the United States. Therefore, all of the discussion on the benefits of cloning is hypothetical. Would actual research prove the hypothetical benefits to be possible? We do not know.

CHAPTER

What Reasonable Conclusions Are Possible?

By this stage, you should be better equipped to pan for intellectual gold—to distinguish stronger reasons from weaker ones.

Consider the following argument:

> Large corporations spend far too much time and money advertising to children. Children's programming is riddled with commercials trying to sell them the latest toy, telling the children they will not be happy unless they have it. The practice of advertising to children is horrendous and should be illegal. Advertising to children, who cannot critically evaluate the ads they see, puts a strain on parents to either say "no" to their children and have them get upset, or to give in to their children's demands, ultimately spoiling the children.

Should you urge your local congressman to criminalize advertisements to children? Suppose you checked the author's reasons and found them believable. Are there other conclusions that might be as consistent with these reasons as the author's conclusion? This chapter will suggest several possible alternative conclusions.

Very rarely will you have a situation in which only one conclusion can be reasonably inferred. In Chapter 9, we discussed the importance of rival causes. The point there was that there are different possible causal bases for a particular causal conclusion. This chapter, however, focuses on the alternative *conclusions* that are all possible outcomes from a single set of reasons.

Consequently, you must make sure that the conclusion you eventually adopt is the most reasonable and the most consistent with your value preferences. Once you find alternative conclusions, you will be better prepared to discover a stronger conclusion from among the enlarged number of options.

Critical Question: ***What reasonable conclusions are possible?***

ASSUMPTIONS AND MULTIPLE CONCLUSIONS

Evidence attempting to support a factual claim or a group of strong reasons supporting a prescriptive conclusion can both be interpreted to mean different things. Reasons do not generally speak for themselves in an obvious way. As we have seen many times, conclusions are reached only after someone makes certain interpretations or assumptions concerning the meaning of the reasons.

If you make a different assumption concerning the meaning of the reasons, you will reach different conclusions. Because we all possess different levels of perceptual precision, frames of reference, and prior knowledge, we repeatedly disagree about which assumptions are preferable. We form different conclusions from reasons because our diverse backgrounds and goals cause us to be attracted to different assumptions when we decide to link reasons to conclusions.

DICHOTOMOUS THINKING: IMPEDIMENT TO CONSIDERING MULTIPLE CONCLUSIONS

Very few important questions can be answered with a simple "yes" or an absolute "no." When people think in black or white, yes or no, right or wrong, or correct or incorrect terms, they engage in *dichotomous thinking*. This type of thinking assumes there are only two possible answers to a question that actually has multiple potential answers. This habit of seeing and referring to *both* sides of a question as if there are only two has devastatingly destructive effects on our thinking. By restricting the conclusions we consider to be only two, we are sharply reducing the robust possibilities that careful reasoning can produce.

We encountered dichotomous thinking earlier when we discussed the either-or fallacy. This fallacy, and dichotomous thinking in general, damages reasoning by overly restricting our vision. We think we are finished after considering two optional decisions, thereby overlooking many options and the positive consequences that could have resulted from choosing one of them.

Dichotomous thinkers often are rigid and intolerant because they fail to understand the importance of context for a particular answer. To see this point more clearly, imagine this situation:

Your roommate asks you to help plan her biology paper. The paper is to address the question, "Should scientists pursue stem cell research?" In her mind, the paper requires her to defend a "yes" or "no" position.

You have learned that dichotomous thinking can be avoided by qualifying conclusions, by putting them into context. This qualification process requires you to ask about any conclusion:

1. *When* is it accurate?
2. *Where* is it accurate?
3. *Why* or *for what purpose* is it accurate?

You then begin to apply this process to the paper assignment.

Would you be surprised by your roommate's growing frustration as you explained that at certain specified times, in certain situations, to maximize particular values or objectives one should allow stem cell research? She's looking for "yes" or "no"; you provided a complicated "it depends on . . ."

Rigid, dichotomous thinking limits the range of your decisions and opinions. Even worse, it overly simplifies complex situations. As a consequence, dichotomous thinkers are high-risk candidates for confusion.

The next section illustrates the restrictive effects of dichotomous thinking.

TWO SIDES OR MANY?

Before we look at several arguments in which multiple conclusions are possible, let's make sure you appreciate the large number of conclusions that are possible with respect to most important controversies. Here are two contemporary questions.

1. Should the United States engage in peacekeeping in other countries?
2. Is William Shakespeare the best playwright of all time?

At first glance, these questions and many like them seem to call for yes or no answers. However, a qualified "yes" or "no" is often the best answer. The advantage of *maybe*, or *it depends on*, as an answer is that it forces you to admit that you do not yet know enough to make a definite answer. But at the same time you avoid a definite answer, you form a tentative decision or opinion that calls for commitment and eventual action. It's wise to seek additional information that would improve the support for your opinions, but at some point you must stop searching and make a decision, even when the most forceful answer you are willing to defend is a "yes, but . . ."

Glance back at the two questions that preceded the previous paragraph. Ask yourself what conclusions would be possible in response to each question. Naturally, a simple "yes" or a "no" answer would be two possible conclusions. Are there others? Yes, there are many! Let's look at just a few of the possible answers to the first of these questions.

Should the United States Engage in Peacekeeping in Other Countries?

1. Yes, when the country is intricately tied to the United States, such as Saudi Arabia.
2. Yes, if the United States is to be perceived as the sole superpower responsible for maintaining world peace.
3. Yes, if the United States' role is to be limited to keeping peace and does not involve fighting a war.
4. Yes, when our economic interests abroad are at stake.
5. No, the United States has enough domestic problems to handle such that we should not spend time in other countries.

Notice that in each case we added a condition necessary before the conclusion can be justified. In the absence of any data or definitions, any of these seven conclusions could be most reasonable. These five are just a few of the conclusions possible for the first question.

SEARCHING FOR MULTIPLE CONCLUSIONS

This section contains one argument pointing out multiple conclusions that could be created from its reasons. The intention is to give you a model to use when you search for conclusions. We will give you the structure of the argument before we suggest alternative conclusions. Study the reasons without looking at the conclusion, and try to identify as many conclusions as possible that would follow from the reasons. You can always use the "when," "where," and "why" questions to help generate alternative conclusions.

CONCLUSION: *The United States should continue to use the death penalty as a form of punishment.*

REASONS:
1. *Without the death penalty, there is no way to punish people who commit wrongs, such as harming guards or inmates, after already having a life sentence.*
2. *It is only fair that someone should die for purposely taking the life of another.*

Let's start by accepting these reasons as sensible to us. What do we then make of them? We have one answer in the conclusion of the writer: Continue the use of the death penalty.

But even when we accept these two reasons, we would not necessarily conclude the same thing. Other conclusions make at least as much sense on the basis of this support. For example, it would follow that we should continue to use the death penalty, but only in cases where someone has already been sentenced to life in prison, and the prisoner kills a guard or another inmate.

Alternatively, these reasons might suggest that we need to maintain the death penalty in cases of prisoners' harming guards or other prisoners. Not only is this alternative conclusion logically supported by the reasons, but it also leads to a conclusion quite different from the original conclusion.

PRODUCTIVITY OF IF-CLAUSES

If you go back over all the alternative conclusions discussed in this chapter, you will notice that each optional conclusion is possible because we are missing certain information, definitions, assumptions, or the frame of reference of the person analyzing the reasons. Consequently, we can create multiple conclusions by the judicious use of *if-clauses.* In an if-clause, we state a condition that we are assuming in order to enable us to reach a particular conclusion. Notice that the use of if-clauses permits us to arrive at a conclusion without pretending that we know more than we actually do about a particular controversy.

When you use if-clauses to precede conclusions, you are pointing out that your conclusion is based on particular claims or assumptions about which you are uncertain. To see what we mean, look at the following sample conditional statements that might precede conclusions.

1. If the tax cut is targeted toward those at the lower end of the economic spectrum, then . . .
2. If a novel contains an easily identifiable protagonist, a clear antagonist, and a thrilling climax, then . . .
3. If automakers can make cars that are more fuel efficient, then . . .

Generating if-clauses is especially helpful in determining reasonable conclusions for evaluative arguments, such as those evaluating the quality of music, art, colleges, or a president's speech, because such arguments require taking a position on what criteria to use for making the evaluations.

If-clauses present you with multiple conclusions that you should assess before making up your mind about the controversy, and they also broaden the list of possible conclusions from which you can choose your` own position.

ALTERNATIVE SOLUTIONS AS CONCLUSIONS

We frequently encounter issues posed in the following form:

Should we do X? Is X desirable?

Such questions naturally "pull" for dichotomous thinking. Often, however, posing questions in this manner hides a broader question, "What should we do about Y?" (usually some pressing problem). Rewording the question in this way leads us to generate multiple conclusions of a particular form: solutions to the problem raised by the reasons. Generating multiple solutions greatly increases the flexibility of our thinking.

Let's examine the following passage to illustrate the importance of generating multiple solutions as possible conclusions.

> Should we close the bars downtown? The answer is a resounding yes! Since the bars opened, a dozen young college students have suffered from alcohol poisoning.

Once we change this question to, "What should we do about the number of college students suffering from alcohol poisoning?" a number of possible solutions come to mind, which help us formulate our conclusion to the issue. For example, we might conclude: "No, we should not close the bars downtown; rather, we should strictly enforce the drinking age and fine bars that sell alcoholic beverages to minors."

When reasons in a prescriptive argument are statements of practical problems, look for different solutions to the problems as possible conclusions.

Clues for Identifying Alternative Conclusions

1. Try to identify as many conclusions as possible that would follow from the reasons.
2. Use *if-clauses* to qualify alternative conclusions.
3. Reword the issue to "What should we do about Y?"

THE LIBERATING EFFECT OF RECOGNIZING ALTERNATIVE CONCLUSIONS

If logic, facts, or studies were self-explanatory, we would approach learning in a particular manner. Our task would be to have someone else, a teacher perhaps, provide the beliefs that we should have. Specifically, we would seek that single identifiable set of beliefs that logic and facts dictate.

While we have tremendous respect for logic and facts, we cannot unduly exaggerate their worth as guides to forming a conclusion. They take us only so far; then we have to go the rest of the way toward belief, using the help that facts and logic have provided.

A first step in using the help that facts and logic provide is the search for possible multiple conclusions consistent with logic and the facts as we know them. This search liberates us in an important way. It frees us from the inflexible mode of learning sketched above. Once we recognize the variety of possible conclusions, each of us can experience the excitement of enhanced personal choice.

ALL CONCLUSIONS ARE NOT CREATED EQUAL

We want to warn you that the rewarding feeling that often comes with generating multiple conclusions may tempt you to treat them as equally credible and to believe your job is done after you've made your list. But remember that some conclusions can be better justified than others, and the most believable conclusions should be the ones that most affect your reaction to the author's reasoning. Indeed, one clever way to weaken strong reasoning about global warming or the cause of the war in Iraq or the wisdom of distance learning is to make the claim that experts disagree.

The implication of such a statement is that once disagreement is identified, one argument is as good as the next. Therefore, there is no basis for new action to address the problem. But such an approach is insulting to careful critical thinking. Critical thinkers have standards of careful reasoning that they can apply to identify the strongest reasoning.

SUMMARY

Very rarely do reasons mean just one thing. After evaluating a set of reasons, you still must decide what conclusion is most consistent with the best reasons in the controversy. To avoid dichotomous thinking in your search for the strongest conclusion, provide alternative contexts for the conclusions through the use of "when," "where," and "why" questions.

Qualifications for conclusions will move you away from dichotomous thinking. If-clauses provide a technique for expressing these qualifications.

For instance, let's take another look at the argument for restricting advertisements aimed at children at the beginning of the chapter. What alternative conclusions might be consistent with the reasons given?

AUTHOR'S CONCLUSION: *Advertisements aimed at children should be illegal.*

ALTERNATIVE CONCLUSIONS:

1. *If corporations are to be treated as persons, then they have a right to free speech that includes advertisements; thus, their right to advertise should not be limited.*
2. *If it can be demonstrated that children are unable to assess what they view, and thus are heavily influenced by the advertisements they see, then advertisements aimed at children should be illegal.*
3. *If the purpose of the proposed legislation is to limit the content of advertisements aimed at children, then the government should not make*

such ads illegal, but rather take a more proactive role in regulating the content of advertisements aimed at children.

Many additional alternative conclusions are possible in light of the author's reasons. We would shrink the quality of our decision making if we did not consider those alternative conclusions as possible bases for our own beliefs.

PRACTICE EXERCISES

? *Critical Question:* ***What reasonable conclusions are possible?***

For each of the following arguments, identify different conclusions that could be drawn from the reasons.

Passage 1

Feeding large numbers of people is not easy. However, dining halls on campus should try to accommodate a larger variety of tastes. Students all across campus consistently complain not only about the quality of food but also about the lack of selection they find in the dining halls. All that the dining halls need to do is offer a wider range of food to better please more students, and thus keep more of them eating on campus as opposed to eating off campus. Dining services are failing in their duty to the students when they do not provide a large selection of food options every day.

Passage 2

I have never been that strong a runner, but when I bought my new training shoes, Mercury, my running time greatly improved. Now I can run faster and longer, and am less sore afterward. *Runner's Digest* also says the Mercury is one of the best shoes on the market. Therefore, all people who want to run should buy Mercury shoes.

Passage 3

For gay and lesbians teens, coming out to family members can be a stressful and emotional process. Recent research shows that family acceptance and support helps these teens avoid depression and suicide. In a survey of 245 gay, lesbian, bisexual, and transgender adolescents and their relatives, those whose families were most supportive, such as parents openly discussing their child's sexual orientation, were half as likely to have reported depressive symptoms in the previous six months of the study compared with teens whose families were less accepting.

Sample Responses

Passage 1

CONCLUSION: *Dining services are not doing an adequate job of providing food on campus.*

REASONS:

1. *Students are upset about the quality of the food.*
2. *There are not enough options provided every day.*
3. *More options would keep students happy and keep them eating on campus.*

To work on this particular critical-thinking skill, we need to assume that the reasons are strong. If we accept these reasons as reliable, we could also reasonably infer the following conclusions:

> If dining services' goal is to provide a wide selection of food while ensuring the least amount of wasted food at the end of the day, then they are not letting students down with the current selections offered to students.
>
> If dining services aim to keep the price of on-campus food down, and a more expansive menu would cause an increase in prices, they are not failing in their duty to students.

Notice that the alternative conclusions put dining services in quite a different light compared to the negative portrayal they received in the original conclusion.

Passage 2

CONCLUSION: *All potential runners should buy Mercury brand shoes.*

REASONS:

1. *When the author bought Mercury brand shoes, her running time greatly improved.*
2. *Runner's Digest stated that Mercury brand shoes are some of the best running shoes on the market.*

First note that the term *all* suggests a likely overgeneralization by the writer and the need for qualifying terms.

On the basis of these reasons, we could infer several reasonable conclusions:

(1) Runners who are similar to the author should consider buying Mercury brand running shoes.

(2) If one can afford Mercury brand shoes, the shoes are a great choice for people who are trying to run faster and longer.

(3) If a runner is unhappy with the shoes she currently uses for training, then it is possible that buying Mercury brand running shoes will improve her running.

FINAL WORD

Critical thinking is a tool. It does something for you. In serving this function for you, critical thinking can perform well or not so well. We want to end this book by urging you to get optimal use of the attitudes and skills of critical thinking that you have worked so hard to develop.

How can you give others the sense that your critical thinking is a friendly tool, one that can improve the lives of the listener and the speaker, the reader and the writer? Like other critical thinkers, we are always struggling with this question. But the one strategy we find most useful is to voice your critical questions as if you are curious. Nothing is more deadly to the effective use of critical thinking than an attitude of, "Aha, I caught you making an error."

As a parting shot, we want to encourage you to engage with issues. Critical thinking is not a sterile hobby, reserved only for classrooms, for taking exams, or for showing off your mental cleverness. It provides a basis for a partnership for action among the reasonable. Beliefs are wonderful, but their payoff is in our subsequent behavior. After you have found the best answer to a question, act on that answer. Make your critical thinking the basis for the creation of an identity of which you can be proud. Put it to work for yourself and for the community in which you find yourself.

We look forward to benefiting from what you have learned.

INDEX

R

S

T